CAVENDISH PRA

County Court Procedure

THIRD EDITION

STEPHEN M GERLIS
DISTRICT JUDGE
BARNET COUNTY COURT

SERIES EDITOR
CM BRAND, SOLICITOR

Cavendish
Publishing
Limited

London • Sydney

Third edition first published in Great Britain 2001 by Cavendish Publishing Limited, The Glass House, Wharton Street, London WC1X 9PX

Telephone: +44 (0)20 7278 8000   Facsimile: +44 (0)20 7278 8080

Email: info@cavendishpublishing.com

Website: www.cavendishpublishing.com

Gerlis, SM

County court procedure – 3rd ed – (Practice notes series)

1 County courts – England   2 County courts – Wales

I Title

347.4'2'02

ISBN 1 85941 309 9

Printed and bound in Great Britain

Contents

1 Introduction to the Civil Procedure Rules

1.1 Design of the scheme

- The new arrangement consists of a set of Civil Procedure Rules (CPR, referred to in this work thus: 'rule 3.4'), a Schedule to the Rules, Practice Directions (referred to in this book as, for example, '27PD3.4') and new forms. The Rules themselves are divided into Parts.

- Such old rules of the High Court and the County Court as still apply are contained in a Schedule to the Rules.

- Except where otherwise provided, the new provisions replace the existing rules in both the County Court and the High Court and the Civil Division of the Court of Appeal. Regard should be had to rule 2.1 as to what matters are covered under the new rules.

- Rules as to enforcement of judgment have not been changed.

1.2 Transitional arrangements (Part 51 and PD)

The new rules apply to all cases issued from 26 April 1999. If a case which started before 26 April 1999 had not come to the court's attention by 25 April 2000, it will have been automatically stayed, unless a trial date had been fixed for the case by that date or there was an outstanding prognosis in a personal injury case, or it was a case concerning trusts.

An application for the stay to be lifted can be made, but, if granted, it will be on terms that the case will continue under the CPR (51PD19). The lifting of the stay will not be automatic and the court will look at all the circumstances to see whether or not the case ought to be allowed to continue.

1.3   The overriding objective

This applies to *all* cases as from 26 April 1999. Rule 1.1(1) states as follows:

> The Rules are a new procedural code with the overriding objective of enabling the court to deal with cases justly.

1.3.1 Practical implications

Pre-26 April 1999 cases are not going to be of much assistance in applications taking place now. Note *Shikari v Malik* (1999) *The Times*, 20 May, in which the Court of Appeal said that litigants whose actions had commenced before the new rules came into force cannot rely on the assumption that what had been tolerated in the past would be tolerated in the future. A similar view was expressed by the Court of Appeal in *Biguzzi v Rank Leisure plc* [1999] 1 WLR 1926. The Court of Appeal also seems to be taking the view that even current cases may not be of much help, as each case is likely to depend on its own circumstances and the application of proportionality to that particular case.

1.4   Proportionality

When exercising any power under the rules or interpreting the Rules, the court must give effect to the overriding objective (rule 1.2) and expect to be helped in this by the parties (rule 1.3).

In order to achieve the overriding objective as set out in rule 1.1 above, rule 1.1(2) states that this includes:

(a) ensuring that the parties are on an equal footing;

(b) saving expense;

(c) dealing with the case in ways which are *proportionate* –

    (i)   to the amount of money involved;

    (ii)   to the importance of the case;

    (iii)   to the complexity of the issues; and

    (iv)   to the financial position of each party;

(d) ensuring that it is dealt with expeditiously and fairly; and

(e) allotting to it an appropriate share of the court's resources, while taking into account the need to allot resources to other cases.

1.4.1 Practical implications

Proportionality pervades all of the rules, but especially with regard to costs and disclosure. Note that, as a result of sub-para (e) above, proportionality is both a subjective and an objective test.

1.5 The 'tracks'

A three tiered system has been introduced governed principally by monetary value. By far the largest number of cases fall into the small claims track, which, broadly, covers claims up to £5,000 (with the exception of personal injuries and housing disrepair cases, where the limit is £1,000) (see below, Chapter 11). The fast track deals with cases between £5 and £15,000 *where the time estimate is no longer than a day* (see below, Chapter 12) and the multi-track is for cases above that level and any others which do not fall within the other two tracks (see below, Chapter 13).

Cases can only be issued in the High Court if they have a value of £15,000 or more (other than personal injuries, where the limit is £50,000 or more) (see below, Chapter 4).

1.5.1 Practical implications

Nearly 90% of civil work falls into the small claims category, with only about 4% falling into the multi-track.

1.6 Case management

Cases at all levels are now principally managed by the courts, not the lawyers, with controlled timetables and trial dates fixed at an early stage (see below, Chapter 10).

Rule 1.4 provides that case management will also be used to further the overriding objective. This includes (rule 1.4(2)):

(a) encouraging the parties to co-operate with each other in the conduct of the proceedings;

(b) identifying the issues at an early stage;

(c) deciding promptly which issues need full investigation and trial and accordingly disposing summarily of the others;

(d) deciding the order in which issues are to be resolved;

(e) encouraging the parties to use an alternative dispute resolution procedure if the court considers that appropriate and facilitating the use of such procedure;

(f) helping the parties to settle the whole or part of the case;

(g) fixing timetables or otherwise controlling the progress of the case;

(h) considering whether the likely benefits of taking a particular step justify the cost of taking it;

(i) dealing with as many aspects of the case as it can on the same occasion;

(j) dealing with the case without the parties needing to attend at court;

(k) making use of technology; and

(l) giving directions to ensure that the trial of a case proceeds quickly and efficiently.

1.6.1 Practical implications

Practitioners will find the courts much more proactive in managing cases. Although the courts may take account of agreed directions, they are not bound to and will endeavour to ensure that cases come on for hearing as soon as possible, with a careful eye kept on costs.

1.7 The Human Rights Act 1998

As of 2 October 2000, the Human Rights Act 1998 came into force. This incorporates the European Convention on Human Rights into the legislation of England and Wales. The courts, as 'public authorities', will be required to give effect to the provisions of the Convention in their deliberations. As the CPR were written with the Convention in mind, it is not anticipated that there will be much that the Convention can add to our existing practice and procedure. In any event, Lord Woolf has twice warned against overuse of the Act – first when sitting as Master of the Rolls in *Daniels v Walker* (2000) 19 Busy Solicitors Digest (BSD) 51 and then at a press conference after being sworn in as Lord Chief Justice ((2000) 19 BSD 151). Areas which may be vulnerable, however, to challenges under Art 6 of the ECHR (the right to a fair trial) may include public hearings, sanctions and fees.

As for setting out a claim when seeking a remedy under the Human Rights Act, see 16PD16.

2 Personnel of the Court

2.1 General

The officers of the county court are the following: circuit judge and district judge, comprising the judicial officers, and court manager (formerly known as the 'chief clerk') and staff who are the administrative or court officers. In addition, part time judges, such as deputy district judges, deputy circuit judges and recorders, may also preside.

2.2 Circuit judges

Circuit judges are assigned by s 5 of the County Courts Act 1984 to sit in county courts. Section 37 of the 1984 Act, set out below, vests them with their powers and gives them authority of jurisdiction:

37(1)   Any jurisdiction and powers conferred by this or any other Act:

(a) on a county court; or

(b) on the judge of a county court;

may be exercised by any judge of the court.

(2)   Subsection (1) applies to jurisdiction and power conferred on all county courts or judges of county courts or on any particular county court or the judge of any particular county court.

The judges also have a general ancillary jurisdiction as provided in s 38 of the 1984 Act, set out below:

38(1)   Subject to what follows, in any proceedings in a county court the court may make any order which could be made by the High Court if the proceedings were in the High Court.

(2)   Any order made by a county court may be –

   (a) absolute or conditional;

   (b) final or interlocutory.

(3)   A county court shall not have power –

   (a) to order freezing or search orders [see below, Chapter 14]; or

   (b) to make any order of a prescribed kind. [However, there is an exception in the case of the Business List in the Central London County Court.]

The procedure in cases before judges is as prescribed by the rules made pursuant to s 75 of the 1984 Act and the CPR 1998. Where no specific procedure is provided by these rules, the general principles of practice in the High Court may be adopted (s 76) by the circuit judge or district judge. For proceedings under certain Acts, procedures may be prescribed by special rules, for example, the Adoption Rules 1984 (SI 1984/265).

The mode of address for circuit judges and recorders sitting in court or in chambers is 'Your Honour'; the correct method of describing them in the lists is given in *Practice Direction* [1982] 1 WLR 101, CA.

2.3   District judges

District judges are appointed by the Lord Chancellor pursuant to s 6 of the 1984 Act and are addressed as 'Sir' or 'Madam'. Their jurisdiction according to the Practice Direction with the CPR is as follows:

A district judge may make an injunction in proceedings which he or she otherwise has jurisdiction to hear. These include:

•   Any claim allocated or allocatable to the small claims or fast track.

•   Proceedings for the recovery of land.

•   By consent of the parties – this includes making, varying and discharging an injunction.

•   Ancillary to a charging order.

•   Ancillary to an order appointing a receiver by way of equitable execution.

•   Order restraining receipt of Crown debt (RSC Ord 77 r 16).

A district judge may not commit a person to prison where a statute gives jurisdiction. Such statutes include s 23 of the Attachments of Earnings Act 1971; s 14 of the Contempt of Court Act 1981 (various contempts of court); ss 152–57 of the Housing Act 1996 (anti-social behaviour); s 3 of the Protection from Harassment Act 1997; and Part IV of the Family Law Act 1996 (domestic violence proceedings).

A district judge has jurisdiction to hear the following:

- any claim allocated to the small claims or the fast track;
- any claim treated as being allocated to the multi-track under r 8.9(c) and Table 2 of the Practice Direction to Part 8. Mortgagees' and landlords' claims for the recovery of land fall within this provision;
- the assessment of damages ('disposal hearings') without financial limit;
- with the consent of the parties and the designated circuit judge (see below, Chapter 13), any other matter.

The district judge will normally hear all applications in the course of proceedings, whether made before or after judgment, unless the circuit judge otherwise directs. Normally, such hearings will be in chambers (see Part 23 of the CPR and below, Chapter 15).

2.4   Deputy district judges

Deputy district judges (appointed under s 8 of the 1984 Act) exercise the full jurisdiction and powers of a district judge, except in relation to applications under the Children Act 1989, where the Family Proceedings (Allocation to Judiciary) Directions 1993 (as amended in 1994) restrict them to hearing interlocutory matters (other than without notice applications) and unopposed trials, and in relation to committals under Part IV of the Family Act 1996 or the Protection from Harassment Act 1997.

A deputy district judge may not (unlike a full district judge) exercise the powers of a district judge when sitting in a court in a district to which he is not appointed (contrast ss 6(5) and 8(1) of the 1984 Act).

2.5   Court manager and 'proper officer'; devolution to administrative staff

Section 75(3)(d) of the 1984 Act provides that the rules made thereunder may prescribe cases in which:

(a) the jurisdiction or powers of a county court or the judge of a county court may be exercised by a district judge or some other officer of the court; or

(b) the jurisdiction or powers of the district judge of a county court may be exercised by some other officer of the court.

The County Court Rules 1981 recognise that the court manager performs most of the functions assigned by the former rules to the district judge, except those of a purely judicial nature. Accordingly, except in the judicial context, the term 'district judge' is replaced in the 1981 Rules by 'proper officer', which is defined (Ord 1 r 3) as the district judge or, in relation to any act of a formal or administrative nature, the chief clerk or any other officer of the court acting on his behalf. There is a saving for acts which are by statute the responsibility of the district judge, such as the keeping of records under s 12 of the 1984 Act.

However, in some cases, the rules go beyond allowing officers of the court to perform acts of a formal or administrative nature, particularly with regard to the enforcement of judgments.

2.6   Solicitors

Solicitors advise and represent litigants before the court. providing a channel of communication between the court and the parties to the proceedings, as well as between the parties themselves. As for solicitors signing statements of case, see below, Chapter 4; for service on solicitors, see below, Chapter 6.

2.6.1 Change of solicitor

Rule 42.1(1) of the CPR 1998 applies where a party wants to change his solicitor, either appointing another or acting in person. In all such cases, the party concerned must file a Notice of Change, serving it on every other party, including the previous solicitor, if there was one.

A form is provided by the Practice Direction. Note that a Notice is required where a solicitor has been acting for an assisted person and the legal aid certificate has been revoked or discharged, his retainer terminated or the assisted person wishes someone else to act for them (42PD2.2).

Former solicitors are considered as continuing to act unless and until the requisite Notice has been served or an order has been made under rule 42.3(1), declaring that the solicitor has ceased to act. Such an order can be made following an application by the solicitor and has to be supported by evidence (rule 42.3(2)). There is no indication in the Rules or Practice Directions as to what evidence is needed. However, it would appear that such an application may be dealt with without the need for a hearing, unless the matter is complex (*Miller v Allied Sainif (UK) Ltd* (2000) *The Times*, 31 October, Ch D (Neuberger J)).

2.7 Rights of audience

Sections 27 and 28 of the Courts and Legal Services Act 1990 contain a comprehensive code relating to rights of audience. None of s 28 and only parts of s 27 has been brought into force, and they are reproduced in *The County Court Practice* in the note to s 60 of the 1984 Act. Suitably qualified and admitted solicitors and barristers have rights of audience and the right to conduct litigation, as do the parties themselves.

Section 60(2) of the 1984 Act, in relation to county courts, provides that, in actions brought by local authorities for possession of a house and/or the recovery of rent or other sum claimed in respect of any persons in occupation of such house, then, insofar as the proceedings are heard by the district judge, any authorised officer of the authority may address the district judge.

A Lord Chancellor's *Practice Direction*, dated 27 January 1978, provides that Fellows of the Institute of Legal Executives, employed in giving assistance in the conduct of litigation to solicitors, may address the court where those solicitors are acting in unopposed applications for an adjournment, or to obtain judgment by consent (unless, notwithstanding the consent, a question arises as to the applicant's entitlement to the judgment or its terms).

Solicitors' clerks are allowed to address the district judge on applications (s 27(2)(e) of the Courts and Legal Services Act 1990), and usually on small claims, in chambers.

It has been held that unrepresented litigants are entitled to an assistant in civil proceedings: *R v Leicester City JJ ex p Barrow* [1991] 3 All ER 935, on the understanding that the assistant is there to assist and not to address the court (*MacKenzie v MacKenzie* [1970] 3 All ER 1034, CA). A litigant in person is entitled to have the proper assistance of a friend even if the hearing is in chambers (*In Re H (A Minor) (Chambers Proceedings: McKenzie Friend)* (1997) *The Times*, 6 May, CA), except in family matters (*R v Bow County Court ex p Pelling* (1999) NLD, 1 March, Div Ct). Except in relation to the special rules applying to lay representatives in small claims matters (see below, Chapter 11), an application for rights of audience by a layperson on behalf of a litigant in person should only be granted in exceptional circumstances (*D v S (Rights of Audience)* (1997) *The Times*, 1 January).

As for representation by a lay representative or on behalf of a company at a small claims hearing, see below, Chapter 11. The court may allow an authorised employee of a company or corporation to address the court.

3 Pre-Action Protocols and ADR

3.1 Pre-action protocols

3.1.1 General

The introduction of pre-action protocols as part of the civil justice reforms is a crucial element in the concept of quick and economic justice. They provide for much of the work involved in preparing cases to be done prior to the issue of proceedings, or 'front-loaded', as this practice is otherwise known.

As yet, only two pre-action protocols exist, one for personal injuries and the other for clinical disputes (formerly known as 'medical negligence'). Others are in the course of preparation.

Even if a protocol does not exist for the type of action in question, the Practice Direction to the Rules on *Protocols* contains a form of protocol to cover those matters:

> In cases not covered by any approved protocol, the court will expect the parties, in accordance with the overriding objective and the matters referred to in rule 1.1(2)(a), (b) and (c), to act reasonably in exchanging information and documents relevant to the claim and generally in trying to avoid the necessity for the start of proceedings.

3.1.2 Personal injury protocol

The personal injury protocol is designed primarily for road traffic accidents, tripping and slipping accidents and accidents at work that are likely to be allocated to the fast track, because time is of the essence in these cases (PD2.3). Industrial diseases are not included (notes of Guidance 2.2).

As for multi-track cases, the spirit if not the letter of the protocol is to be followed, especially because of the 'cards on the table' approach to litigation enshrined in the changes (PD 2.4).

3.1.3 Procedure

Letter of claim (for specimen, see Appendix A to Protocol) (PD3)

(a) Two copies to be sent to defendant 'immediately sufficient information is available to substantiate a realistic claim and before issues of quantum are addressed in detail' (PD3.1).

(b) Contents of letter of claim (PD3.2–3.5):
- clear summary of facts;
- indication of nature of injuries;
- indication of financial loss;
- request for details;
- sufficient information to enable defendant to commence investigations and put a broad valuation on the risk.

After the defendant has made clear his position on liability, the claimant must provide details of special damages as soon as possible (PD3.13).

Defendant's response

(a) Defendant to reply and to identify insurer (if any) within 21 days (PD3.6).

(b) Insurers must reply within three months, stating whether liability is denied, and, if so, giving reasons for their denial of liability (PD3.7).

(c) Formal admissions will be binding in cases up to £15,000 (PD3.9).

The documents

If the defendant denies liability, this must be accompanied with documents in the defendant's possession that are 'material' to the issues (PD3.10). A list of specimen documents is given in the protocol (Appendix B to Protocol) (PD3.11).

Where the defendant admits primary liability but alleges contributory negligence by the claimant, reasons and material documents must be supplied. The claimant should reply to the allegation before proceedings are issued (PD3.12).

Instructing the expert

Before instructing an expert, the claimant must send to the defendant a list of experts, and the defendant has 14 days to object to any or all of them (PD3.14, 3.16). If they object only to some, the claimant should use a mutually acceptable one (PD3.16). If there is objection to all of them, then the claimant may instruct an expert of their own choice and the claimant does not have to disclose the report prior to proceedings, save where there is an admission (PD3.17).

If the defendant raises no objections, they lose the right to instruct their own expert, unless the first party agrees, the court so directs or the first party refuses to disclose the original of a report that has been amended (PD3.18).

A draft letter of instruction is included with the protocol (specimen letter of instruction to medical expert – Appendix C) (PD3.15).

Agreed questions may be sent to the expert (PD3.19). The cost of the agreed expert's report is borne by the instructing first party; the costs of answering questions is borne by those asking them (PD3.20).

Note PD3.21:

> Where the Defendant admits liability in whole or in part before proceedings are issued, the medical report obtained by agreement should be disclosed to the other party. The claimant should delay issuing proceedings for 21 days from disclosure of the report to enable the parties to consider whether the claim is capable of settlement.

A Part 36 offer (see below, Chapter 20) can be made prior to the issue of proceedings (PD3.21) (and see below, 3.1.5).

3.1.4 Stocktaking

Note PD2.14:

> Where a claim is not resolved when the protocol has been followed, the parties might wish to carry out a stock-take of the issues in dispute, and the evidence that the court is likely to need to decide those issues, *before proceedings are started*. Where the defendant is insured and the pre-action steps have been conducted by the insurer, the insurer would normally be expected to nominate solicitors to act in the proceedings and the claimant's solicitor is recommended to invite the insurer to nominate solicitors to act in the proceedings and do so between 7 and 14 days before the intended issue date.

3.1.5 Settling

Note PD2.13:

> Parties and their legal representatives are encouraged to enter into discussions and/or negotiations prior to starting proceedings. The protocol does not specify when or how this might be done but parties should bear in mind that the courts increasingly take the view that *litigation should be a last resort*, and that claims should not be issued prematurely when a settlement is in reasonable prospect.

3.1.6 Clinical disputes

Procedure

(a) Letter of claim (Appendix C1 to Protocol) (PD3.14–3.22):
- clear summary of the facts;
- main allegation of negligence;
- the patient's injuries;
- financial losses in outline;
- chronology of events in more complex cases;
- reference to any relevant documents, plus copies, if they are not in the defendant's possession;
- offer to settle, if relevant.

(b) Defendants' response (Appendix C2 to Protocol) (PD3.23–27):
- acknowledge within 14 days;
- reasoned answer within three months, with admission or part admission or specific denial, together with documents relied on;
- response to offer to settle.

Experts

PD4.2 states: 'It is recognised that in clinical negligence disputes the parties and their advisers will require flexibility in their approach to expert evidence.'

Expert opinions may be needed on breach of duty and causation; on patient's condition and prognosis; or to assist in valuing the claim.

3.1.7 **Compliance with the protocols**

The standards set in protocols will be 'the normal reasonable approach to pre-action conduct' (Introduction 1.4). The *Practice Direction on Protocols* contains guidance as to compliance:

2.1 The Civil Procedure Rules enable the court to take into account compliance or non-compliance with an applicable protocol when giving directions for the management of proceedings (see rules 3.1(4) and (5) and 3.9(e)) and when making orders for costs (see rule 44.3(5)(a)).

2.2 The court will expect all parties to have complied in substance with the terms of an approved protocol.

2.3 If, in the opinion of the court, non-compliance has led to the commencement of proceedings which might otherwise not have needed to be commenced, or has led to costs being incurred in the proceedings that might otherwise not have been incurred, the orders the court may make include:

(1) an order that the party at fault pay the costs of the proceedings, or part of those costs, of the other party or parties;

(2) an order that the party at fault pay those costs on an *indemnity* basis;

(3) if the party at fault is a claimant in whose favour an order for the payment of damages or some specified sum is subsequently made, an order depriving that party of interest on such sum and in respect of such period as may be specified, and/or awarding interest at a lower rate than that at which interest would otherwise have been awarded;

(4) if the party at fault is a defendant and an order for the payment of damages or some specified sum is subsequently made in favour of the claimant, an order awarding *interest* on such sum and in respect of such period as may be specified at a higher rate, not exceeding 10% above base rate (cf rule 36.21(2)), than the rate at which interest would otherwise have been awarded.

2.4 The court will exercise its powers under paras 2.1 and 2.3 with the object of placing the innocent party in no worse a position than he would have been in if the protocol had been complied with.

As to non-compliance:

3.1 A claimant may be found to have failed to comply with a protocol by, for example:

(a) not having provided sufficient information to the defendant; or

(b) not having followed the procedure required by the protocol to be followed

(eg not having followed the medical expert instruction procedure set out in the Personal Injury Protocol).

3.2 A defendant may be found to have failed to comply with a protocol by, for example:

(a) not making a preliminary response to the letter of claim within the time fixed for that purpose by the relevant protocol (21 days under the Personal Injury Protocol, 14 days under the Clinical Negligence Protocol);

(b) not making a full response within 3 months of the letter of claim, as required by the relevant protocol; or

(c) not disclosing documents required to be disclosed by the relevant protocol,

Practical implications

The court will expect parties to make every effort to settle cases, or at least narrow issues prior to the issue of proceedings. Failure to do so runs the risk of penalties, especially in costs, later on.

When it comes to assessment of costs, the costs rules also provide in addition that, in deciding whether costs were reasonably incurred or are proportionate, the court may take into account the efforts made, if any, before and during the proceedings in order to try to resolve the dispute (see below, Chapter 21). Both sides may make offers to settle at the pre-proceedings stage, with consequent sanctions for failure to accept if the case is unnecessarily prolonged.

3.1.8 Actions to recover costs

Where parties have agreed all matters pre-issue other than the question of costs, rule 44.12A provides a mechanism for bringing proceedings just to recover costs (see below, Chapter 21).

3.2   Alternative dispute resolution

Rule 1. 4 of the CPR provides that the court must further the overriding objective by actively managing cases. Active case management includes:

> (2)(e) Encouraging the parties to use an alternative dispute resolution procedure if the court considers that appropriate and facilitating the use of such procedure ...

The court will do this by either setting up its own schemes, where the budget permits (the Central London County Court has a fast track (£5,000–£15,000) scheme) or by providing information as to where such schemes are available. Rule 26.4(1) enables the court to stay the proceedings for a month (or longer, if the parties agree) while such alternative methods of settling the matter are explored; an invitation to do this is in the Allocation Questionnaire (see below, Chapter 10). Failure to take advantage of such schemes where they are available may be condemned in costs. Financial assistance from the Legal Services Commission is now available to cover mediation.

3.2.1   Practical implications

Apart from the Central London scheme (which is very much under-used), the few alternative dispute resolution (ADR) schemes in existence seem to be more geared to large commercial disputes, for which they are more appropriate. Increased use of ADR for smaller claims will depend upon the establishment of schemes tailored to that level of dispute and the willingness of litigants to submit themselves to them. This may be encouraged by costs implications and pressure by the courts as part of their case management function.

4 General Procedure for Bringing a Claim

4.1 Choice of court

The following must be issued in the *High Court*:

- any claim where the High Court has exclusive jurisdiction by statute (these include a claim for damages or other remedy for libel or slander);
- claims for habeas corpus and judicial review;
- claims needing to be heard in a High Court specialist list.

The following must be issued in a *county court*:

- personal injury claims where the claimant does not expect to recover £50,000 or more;
- other claims where the claimant does not expect to recover £15,000 or more;
- any claim where the county court has exclusive jurisdiction by statute.

Otherwise, a claim may be issued in either court, but, if the claimant believes that it should be dealt with by a High Court judge by reason of its value, complexity or general importance, it should be started in that court.

4.1.1 Chancery business

Chancery business may be commenced in the High Court or the county court, but the upper limit for Chancery business in the county court, referred to in s 23 of the County Courts Act 1984 as 'Equity Jurisdiction', remains at a maximum figure of value of the estate or trust of £30,000. When the county court is used for Chancery business, the Claim Form should be marked, at the top right hand corner, 'Chancery business'.

4.1.2 Complex cases; special enactments

Regardless of value, claims may be started in the High Court if the claimant believes that the claim should be dealt with by a High Court judge by reason of complexity of facts, legal remedies or procedures involved and/or importance to the public (7PD2.4).

Some enactments specifically require commencement in the High Court or in a county court, when the claim must be issued in the court which the enactment specifies.

4.2 Statements of case (Part 16)

'Statement of case' is the new term for a pleading and includes:

- the claim form (see below);
- particulars of claim, where these are not included in a claim form (see below);
- the defence;
- a Part 20 claim;
- reply to the defence; and
- any further information given in relation to them voluntarily or by court order.

4.2.1 Amending the statement of case

A statement of case which *has not yet been served* may always be amended, and no permission is required (rule 17(1)). But note rule 17.2:

(1) If a party has amended his statement of case where permission of the court was not required, the court may disallow the amendment.

(2) A party may apply to the court for an order under paragraph (1) within 14 days of service of a copy of the amended statement of case on him.

If an amendment is required *after service*, an application must be filed, accompanied by the proposed amendment. The application may be dealt with at a hearing, but not if the court considers that a hearing would not be appropriate, or where the parties themselves agree that a hearing is unnecessary, or simply agree the amendment, although this would be subject to scrutiny by the court (rule 23.8 and 17PD1.1).

Any party who seeks permission will find that permission is given subject to directions as to amendments made as to any other statements of case, and as to service. A party applying for an amendment will usually be responsible for the costs of and arising from the amendment. If a statement of case is amended, the statement of truth should be re-verified (17PD1.4). As to amendments made after a limitation period has expired, rule 17.4 states that the court will allow amendments only if there is a new claim arising out of the same facts. An amendment to correct the name of a party after a genuine mistake is allowable, if the court permits, under rule 17.4(3).

4.3 Statement of truth (Part 22)

This is a statement that the party putting forward a document believes it to be true. Thew documents that must be included are:

- statement of case (formerly known as a 'pleading');
- the response to order for further information (which, by virtue of rule 2.3(1), *is* a statement of case);
- a witness statement.

It must be signed by:

- the maker of the statement, if it is a witness statement;
- a party or litigation friend or legal representative (rule 22.1(6)).

Upon failure to provide a statement of truth, the claimant/defendant cannot rely on the document as evidence of any of the matters set out in it, and a statement of case not so verified *may* be struck out (22PD4).

The statement must be in the following form (22PD2):

I believe [or, as the case may be, 'the claimant believes'] that the facts in this [name of document being verified] are true.

If it is a witness statement which is being verified, the wording should be:

I believe that the facts stated in this witness statement are true.

A false statement amounts to a contempt (rule 32.14), so practitioners are advised that only those with direct knowledge of the facts should actually sign the statement of truth, although the form of the statement of truth does allow the signatory to say that 'the claimant believes it to be true'. Practitioners cannot sign a *witness* statement other than their own.

Where a party is legally represented, and the legal representative signs the document, it will be assumed that he explained to the client beforehand the possible consequences if the statement turns out not to be true (22PD3.8). Where a company or corporation is involved, the statement should be signed by a person holding a senior position. In the case of a partnership, a partner or person having control of the business should sign (22PD3). For details of others who may sign the statement of truth, such as insurers, managing agents, trustees, etc, see 22PD3.

Note that the cost of using an affidavit instead of a statement verified under Part 22 can only be recovered if the rule or Practice Direction requires an affidavit. The net result of this is that affidavits are now much less likely to be used.

4.4   The claim form

Subject to an alternative procedure of limited application (Part 8 in the CPR – see below, Chapter 5), all proceedings are now started in all courts by a *claim form*, which may set out the particulars of claim in the space provided on the form. A copy of the claim form appears in the Appendix to this book (Chapter 24). If there is insufficient room on the claim form to set out all the details of the claim, the claimant may use a supplementary document called 'particulars of claim'. If the claimant intends to use particulars of claim, this must be stated on the claim form.

Note the provisions of rule 7.5:

- the particulars of claim must be served on the defendant within 14 days of the service of the claim form but, in any event, no later than the last day for service of the claim form;

- within seven days of service of the particulars of claim, the claimant must file a copy of the Particulars and a certificate of service (rule 6.10 makes provision for certificates of service).

The particulars of claim must, if not accompanying the claim form, be served no later than the latest time for serving the Claim Form, that is, within four months after the date of issue (rule 7.5(1)). Six months is allowed for service out of the jurisdiction, wherever that may be (rule 7.5(3)). Application can be made to extend time for service if made *before* the four months (or six months) has expired (rule7.6(2)), but any application for an order to extend time for service *'must be supported by evidence'* (rule 7.6(4)). Where there is to be service out of the jurisdiction, an endorsement is required (7PD 3.5).

The required contents of the claim form are apparent from the form itself, Practice Form N1, and are given below. The claim form must:

- contain a concise statement of the nature of the claim;
- specify the remedy which the claimant seeks;
- in a money claim, state the value which the claimant places on the claim; and
- contain such other matters as may be set out in a Practice Direction.

4.4.1 Practical implications

As with defences, which are dealt with below in Chapter 7, claims must state in plain English what the dispute is all about. The old practice in some cases, such as road traffic accident cases, of formulaic pleading will no longer be tolerated if it does not explain in simple language both to the court and the defendant what the claim is all about.

In a claim for money, the claim form must also *specify* the amount of money claimed, or, if the claimant is unable to do so, he must state in the claim form that he expects to recover:

- not more than £5,000;
- more than £5,000 but not more than £15,000; or
- more than £15,000.

Alternatively, the claimant may state that he does not know how much he expects to recover.

In a claim which does not exceed £5,000 in value for, or which includes a claim for, personal injury, the claimant must also state the amount he expects to recover as general damages for pain, suffering and loss of amenity. This is relevant on allocation of the claim to a track, should it become defended. If the pain, suffering and loss of amenity element of the claim exceeds £1,000, the claim will not be allocated to the small claims track.

Similarly, in a claim which includes a claim by a tenant of residential premises against his landlord where the tenant is seeking an order that the landlord carry out repairs or other work to the premises, the claimant must state whether the amount of damages he expects to recover for this part of the claim, or any resulting damages claim, exceeds or does not exceed £1,000. Again, if such a claim or resulting claim is expected to exceed £1,000, it will not be allocated to the small claims track, should it become defended.

4.4.2 Specified/unspecified claims

For the purposes of claims brought under the CPR, there is no longer a distinction between 'liquidated' and 'unliquidated' claims. The distinction now is between a claim for 'a specified sum' and a claim for 'an unspecified sum'. The importance of the distinction is in how admissions are dealt with (see below, Chapter 7), and also in connection with the new rules for automatic transfer (see below, Chapter 10).

It is worth noting that a claimant is not bound to only make an unspecified claim in cases where there has previously been an assessment, for example, for personal injuries ('damages not exceeding £X') but can elect to make a specified claim ('damages in the sum of £X') and claim a default judgment (see below) for that sum.

4.5   Contents of particulars of claim

Note rule 16.4:

(1) Particulars of claim must include:

    (a) a concise statement of the facts on which the claimant relies;

    (b) if the claimant's seeking interest, a statement to that effect and the details set out in paragraph (2);

    (c) if the claimant's seeking aggravated damages or exemplary damages, a statement to that effect and his grounds for claiming them;

    (d) if the claimant is seeking provisional damages, a statement to that effect and his grounds for claiming them; and

    (e) such other matters as may be set out in a practice direction.

(2) If the claimant is seeking *interest* he must:

    (a) state whether he is doing so –

        (i)   under the terms of a contract,

        (ii) under an enactment and if so which, or

        (iii) on some other basis and if so what that basis is; and

    (b) if the claim is for a specified amount of money, state –

        (i)   the percentage rate at which interest is claimed,

        (ii) the date from which it is claimed,

        (iii) the date to which it is calculated, which must not be later than the date on which the claim form is issued,

(iv) the total amount of interest claimed to the date of calculation, and

(v) the daily rate at which interest accrues after that date.

Where a claim is made for an injunction or declaration in respect of or relating to any land or the possession, occupation, use or enjoyment of any land, the particulars of claim must:

- state whether or not the injunction or declaration relates to residential premises; and
- identify the land by reference to a plan, where necessary.

Where a claim is brought to enforce a right to recover *possession of goods*, the particulars of claim must contain a statement showing the value of the goods.

Where a claim is based upon a *written agreement*:

- a copy of the contract or documents constituting the agreement should be attached to or served with the particulars of claim and the original(s) should be available at the hearing; and
- any general conditions of sale incorporated in the contract is or the documents constituting the agreement are bulky this Practice Direction is complied with by attaching or serving only the relevant parts of the contract or documents).

Where a claim is based upon an *oral agreement*, the particulars of claim should set out the contractual words used and state by whom, to whom, when and where they were spoken.

Where a claim is based upon an *agreement by conduct*, the particulars of claim must specify the conduct relied on and state by whom, when and where the acts constituting the conduct were done.

4.5.1 Matters relied on which must be specifically set out in the particulars of claim

Note the Practice Direction to Part 16:

A Claimant who wishes to rely on evidence:

(1) under Section 11 of the Civil Evidence Act 1968 of a conviction of an offence, or

(2) under Section 12 of the above-mentioned Act of a finding or adjudication of adultery or paternity, must include in his Particulars of Claim a statement to that effect and give the following details:

(1) the type of conviction, finding or adjudication and its date,

(2) the Court or Court Martial which made the conviction, finding or adjudication, and

(3) the issue in the claim to which it relates.

The Claimant must specifically set out the following matters in his Particulars of Claim where he wishes to rely on them in support of his claim:

(1) any allegation of fraud,

(2) the fact of any illegality,

(3) details of any misrepresentation,

(4) details of all breaches of trust,

(5) notice or knowledge of a fact,

(6) details of unsoundness or mind or undue influence,

(7) details of wilful default, and

(8) any facts relating to mitigation of loss or damage.

Any party may:

- refer in his statement of case to any point of law on which his claim is based;

- give in his statement of case the name of any witness whom he proposes to call; and

- attach to or serve with the statement of case a copy of any document which he considers is necessary to his claim (including any expert's report, to be filed in accordance with Part 35).

4.5.2 Claims in respect of personal injuries (16PD4)

The Practice Direction to Part 16 provides that the Particulars must contain:

(1) The Claimant's date of birth, and

(2) Brief details of the Claimant's personal injuries.

The claimant must attach to his particulars of claim a schedule of details of any past and future expenses and losses which he claims (16PD4.2). If the claimant is relying on the evidence of a medical practitioner, the claimant must attach to or serve with his particulars of claim a report from a medical practitioner about the personal injuries which he alleges in his claim (16PD4.3).

In a *provisional damages claim*, the claimant must state in his particulars of claim (16PD4.4):

(1) That he is seeking an award of provisional damages under either Section 32A of the Supreme Court Act 1091 or Section 51 of the County Courts Act 1984.

(2) That there is a chance that at some future time the Claimant will develop some serious disease or suffer some serious deterioration in his physical or mental condition.

(3) Specify the disease or type of deterioration in respect of which an application may be made at a future date.

In a *fatal accident claim*, the claimant must state in his particulars of claim (16PD5):

(1) that it is brought under the Fatal Accidents Act 1976,

(2) the dependants on whose behalf the claim is made,

(3) the date of birth of each dependant, and

(4) details of the nature of the dependency claim.

In a claim for *recovery of land* (see, also, below, Chapter 5), the particulars of claim must (16PD6):

(1) Identify the land sought to be recovered.

(2) State whether the claim relates to residential premises.

(3) If the claim relates to residential premises, state whether the rateable value of the premises on every day specified by Section 4(2) of the Rent Act 1977 in relation to the premises exceeds the sum so specified or whether the rent for the time being payable in respect of the premises exceeds the sum specified in Section 4(4)(b) of the Act.

(4) Where the claim relates to residential premises and is for non-payment of rent, state:

(a) the amount due at the start of the proceedings,

(b) details of all payments which have been missed,

(c) details of any history of late or under payment,

(d) any previous steps taken to recover the arrears of rent with full details of any Court proceedings, and

(e) any relevant information about the Defendant's circumstances, in particular whether any payments are made on his behalf directly to the Claimant under the Social Security Contributions and Benefits Act 1992.

(5) Give details about the agreement or tenancy, if answer which the land was held, stating when it determined and the amount of money payable by way of rent or licence fee.

(6) In a case to which Section 138 of the County Courts Act 1984 applies (forfeiture for non-payment), state the daily rate at which the rent in arrear is to be calculated.

(7) State the ground on which possession is claimed whether statutory or otherwise.

(8) In a case where the Claimant knows of any person entitled to claim relief against forfeiture as under-lessee (including a mortgagee) under Section 146(4) of the Law of Property Act 1925 (or in accordance with Section 38 of the Supreme Court Act 1981), give the name and address of that person.

Where the claim is for the delivery of goods let under a *hire purchase agreement* to a person other than a company or other corporation, the claimant must state in the particulars of claim (16PD7.1):

(1) the date of the Agreement,

(2) the parties to the Agreement,

(3) the number or other identification of the Agreement,

(4) where the Claimant was not one of the original parties to the Agreement, the means by which the rights and duties of the creditor passed to him,

(5) whether the Agreement is a regulated agreement and if it is not a regulated agreement, the reason why,

(6) the place where the Agreement was signed by the Defendant,

(7) the goods claimed,

(8) the total price of the goods,

(9) the paid-up sum,

(10) the unpaid balance of the total price,

(11) whether a Default Notice or a Notice under Section 76(1) or 98(1) of the Consumer Credit Act 1974 has been served on the Defendant, and if it has, the date and method of service,

(12) the date when the right to demand delivery of the goods accrued,

(13) the amount (if any) claimed as an alternative to the delivery of goods, and

(14) the amount (if any) claimed in addition to:

(a) the delivery of the goods, or

(b) any claim under (13) above, with the grounds of each claim.

Where the claim is not for the delivery of goods, the claimant must state in his particulars of claim (16PD7.2):

- the matters set out in para 8.19(1) to (6) above,

- the goods let under the Agreement,

- the amount of the total price,

- the paid up sum,

- the amount (if any) claimed as being due and unpaid in respect of any instalment or instalments of the total price, and

- the nature and amount of any other claim and how it arises.

4.6 Defamation

Proceedings for defamation may not be started, nor transferred, to the county court save by agreement in writing between the parties. 16PD8 contains the requirements for the contents of the particulars of claim.

4.7 Specialist proceedings

For a definition of this, see Part 49. The claim form N1 cannot always be used, as '*it may be necessary*' to follow the relevant PD and use the Practice Form approved for issue of the particular specialist proceedings, that is, one of those proceedings listed in Parts 49 and 50. The CPR will apply only to the extent that they are not inconsistent with rules and Practice Directions which apply to these specialist claims.

4.8 Children and patients (Part 21)

Once proceedings are started, there must be a 'litigation friend', the new expression for a 'next friend', or 'guardian ad litem' (rule 21.2). A 'child', in the Rules, means a person under 18, referred to in other enactments as a 'minor'. A 'patient' means a person who, by reason of mental disorder within the meaning of the Mental Health Act 1988, is incapable of managing and administering his own affairs (rule 21.1). There is a proviso that the court may make an order permitting a 'child' to conduct proceedings by itself (rule 21.2(3)).

A litigation friend must file the following (rule 21.5):

- his/her authorisation;
- certificate of suitability, that is, can fairly and competently conduct the proceedings and no adverse interest,
- undertaking of claimant to pay costs ordered.

The court's approval of *settlements* is necessary wherever the claimant or any party is a patient or child (rule 21.10). All money is to be paid into the court and will become subject to directions (rule 21.11).

4.9   Addresses and titles

4.9.1 Claimant's address

If not represented by a solicitor, the claimant must give his residence or business address as his address for service. If represented, the solicitor's address will be his address for service (but the claim form itself requires his personal address also to be given). The address for service must be within England or Wales.

4.9.2 Children and patients

A child's name should be followed by '(a child by ... his litigation friend)' or, if a litigation friend is dispensed with, then simply '(a child)'. The name of a party suffering mental disorder should be followed by '(by ... his litigation friend)'.

4.9.3 Firms and other unincorporated bodies

In the county court, the names of individuals and partners suing or sued in their own names may be followed by '(trading as <*firm name*>)' and when suing or sued in the names of the firm or body, the name may be followed by '(a trading name)'. In the High Court, it will be convenient to follow a similar practice, as hitherto.

4.10   Discontinuing a claim (Part 38)

To discontinue a claim or part of a claim, a claimant must (rule 38.3(1)):

* file a notice of discontinuance;
* serve a copy on every other party.

The notice of discontinuance must state that notice on every other party has been served and, where consent of some other party is needed, a copy of that consent must be attached (rule 38.3(2), (3)). The notice must make it clear, if there is more than one defendant, which one the claim is discontinued against (rule 38.3(4)).

4.10.1   Liability for costs

Unless the court orders otherwise, a claimant who discontinues is liable for the costs of the defendant up to the date of service of the notice (rule 38.6(1)). Rule 44.12 provides for the basis of assessment of costs where a claim has been discontinued – basically, this will be on the standard basis. These provisions as to costs do not apply to small claims (rule 38.6(3)).

4.10.2   Stay of proceedings

Where the action has only been partly discontinued, the court may order that the rest of the action remains stayed until the costs are paid (rule 38.8).

5 Part 8 Alternative Procedure

5.1 General

This largely replaces the previous originating summons. Regard should be had to the relevant Tables (see below) and rules to determine whether an action should be commenced using Part 8 rather than Part 7. The claimant must state on the claim form that Part 8 applies, and that he seeks a decision not involving a substantial dispute of fact; or a Practice Direction permits, or requires, 'Part 8 Procedure'. A copy of the Part 8 claim form is given below, Chapter 24.

Note the provisions of rule 8.1(6):

(6) A rule or practice direction may, in relation to a specified type of proceedings:

(a) require or permit the use of the Part 8 procedure; and

(b) disapply or modify any of the rules set out in this Part as they apply to those proceedings.

The claimant must specify (rule 8.2):

- the question to be decided; or
- the remedy sought; and
- the enactment, if any, under which the claim is made.

5.2 Which matters are Part 8?

The Practice Direction to Part 8 gives examples of where the procedure may be used:

1.4 The types of claim for which the Part 8 procedure may be used include:

(1) a claim by or against a child or patient which has been settled before the commencement of proceedings and the sole purpose of the claim is to obtain the approval of the court to the settlement,

(2) a claim for provisional damages which has been settled before the commencement of proceedings and the sole purpose of the claim is to obtain a consent judgment,

(3) an application for a deposition to be taken abroad under Part 34, made other than in existing proceedings,

(4) an application for a deposition to be taken in England and Wales for use before courts abroad, and

(5) provided there is unlikely to be a substantial dispute of fact, a claim for a summary order for possession against named or unnamed defendants occupying land or premises without the licence or consent of the person claiming possession.

Practice Direction 8B sets out a list of all those proceedings where the Part 8 procedure *must* be used. The Direction is divided into three sections: A, B, and C. Section A applies to:

- all claims listed in Table 1 to the Practice Direction;
- claims where an Act provides that an application of claim is to be brought by originating summons; and
- claims or applications which, before 26 April 1999, would have been brought by originating summons, but only if such claim or application is not listed in Section C to the Practice Direction,

provided that no other method of bringing the claim after 26 April 1999 is prescribed in a Schedule, rule or Practice Direction.

The matters listed in Table 1 are all *High Court* matters, and include:

- enforcement of charging orders;
- some applications for reciprocal enforcement of judgments;
- some proceedings by and against the Crown;
- mortgage possession actions;
- proceedings under the Landlord and Tenant Acts 1927, 1954 and 1987;
- applications for possession under RSC Ord 113 (squatters).

Section B applies to:

- all claims listed in Table 2 to the Practice Direction;

- in the *county court*, claims for:
  - o the recovery of possession of land; or
  - o damages for harassment under s 3 of the Protection from Harassment Act 1997;
- claims that before 26 April 1999 would have been brought:
  - o in the High Court by originating motion, but only if not included in Section C to the Practice Direction;
  - o in the county court, by originating application or petition,

  provided that no other procedure is prescribed in an Act, Schedule, rule or Practice Direction.

The matters listed in Table 2 include:

- in the *High Court*:
  - o appeals by case stated under RSC Ord 56 rr 8 and 10;
  - o various other appeals under RSC Ord 94;
  - o references to the European Court;
- in the county court:
  - o summary possession proceedings under CCR Ord 24;
  - o enforcement of charging orders by sale;
  - o applications under the Landlord and Tenant Acts 1927, 1954, 1985 and 1987, including, importantly, applications for a new tenancy under s 24 of the 1954 Act (although it looks as though the old type of claim form can be used for the latter);
  - o certain applications under the Consumer Credit Act 1974;
  - o accelerated possession order applications;
  - o injunction applications under s 152 of the Housing Act 1996.

5.3   Contents of claim

County Court Rules (CCR) Ords 6 and 7 make special provision for the contents of the particulars of claim in certain types of claim and for service of them, and there are also to be found in the CCR further special provisions relating to the venue for bringing proceedings and for periods of notice for hearings. Paragraphs B2 and B3 of the Practice Direction make it clear that such special provisions continue to apply in precedence to the general provisions of Practice Direction 8B. Section C applies to certain appeals in the High Court.

5.4   The procedure

5.4.1 High Court

The main differences between the general procedure under Part 7 (see above, Chapter 4) and the Part 8 (High Court) procedure are:

- the claimant must file and serve any evidence on which he wishes to rely with the claim form;
- an acknowledgment of service *must* be filed;
- the defendant must file and serve any evidence on which he wishes to rely when he files and serves his acknowledgment of service;
- the acknowledgment is served by the defendant;
- a defence is not required;
- default judgment is not available;
- the claim is treated as allocated to the multi-track;
- the claimant must file and serve any evidence in reply within 14 days of service of the defendant's evidence;
- the court may require or permit any party or witness to attend to give oral evidence or to be cross-examined.

The Part 20 (third party and counterclaims) procedure (see below, Chapter 8) applies to Part 8 claims, save that leave is always required to issue.

A defendant may object to the use of the Part 8 procedure and the court has power, whether of its own motion or otherwise, to order that the procedure should cease to apply.

5.4.2 County court

Section B of Practice Direction 8B (county court procedure) varies the general Part 8 procedure described above. The 'variant' element of the procedure is that a date for hearing will be fixed on issue, at least 21 days' notice of which will be required to be given. Section B also provides that an acknowledgment of service is not required to be served, but it would appear that rule 8.4(2) will still apply. This provides that a defendant who has not filed an acknowledgment may attend the hearing but may not take any part in it without the court's permission.

Otherwise, the Part 8 procedure will apply, which includes the filing of evidence on issue for the claimant, and with the acknowledgment of service for the defendant.

Claimants in residential possession cases must use the pre–26 April 1999 forms (N5, N119, N120 – see Practice Direction 8B8(2)). There is no change in the information that must be included in Particulars of Claim (see CCR Ord 6 rr 3 and 5, which are retained in Sched 2 to the CPR) notwithstanding 16PD6/7, which appear to be redundant. As before, on issue the court fixes a date for the hearing (8BPD para B.9) and, except in cases where other rules provide for a shorter period, 21 days' notice of the hearing must be given. At the hearing, the court may hear the case or give directions.

5.4.3 Practical implications

The greatest problem with Part 8 is identifying which matters need to be issued under this provision. The requirements with regard to residential possession proceedings as described above are hardly satisfactory, requiring, as they do, a hybrid system whereby a Part 8 claim form is not actually used but, rather, the old forms. It is hoped that these problems will be solved by the forthcoming review of possession procedure.

Practitioners also need to be reminded that, notwithstanding the use of the old forms in possession matters, they still need to file their evidence, for example, agreements and notices, *at the time of issue,* and not wait until the hearing itself, or shortly beforehand. The defendant is entitled to see that evidence when the claim is served on him. Failure to comply with this may result in adjournments and/or costs sanctions.

6 Service

6.1 General (Part 6)

The court has a general power to dispense altogether with service of any document 'if it is appropriate to do so' (rule 6.9) and application may be made for such an order, without notice. The court may also make an order authorising service by some method not of itself authorised by the rules; an application for such an order can also be made without notice, supported by evidence (6PD9). An order permitting an alternative method of service will specify the method and will state the date when the document will be deemed to be served (rule 6.8).

When solicitors are authorised by their clients to accept service, or hold themselves out as accepting service, then, except in cases where personal service on a party is required by some enactment, by court order or by a Practice Direction, the document must be served on those solicitors.

An enactment, or a rule within the CPR, or a Practice Direction, may make a specific provision and requirement for service; or, in any case at all, the court can order service as it thinks fit. Subject to this, five methods of service are given under rule 6.2(1):

(a) personal service;

(b) first class post;

(c) leaving the document at the party's address for service, namely, his residence or place of business within the jurisdiction, or else the business address of his solicitors;

(d) through a document exchange in accordance with 6PD2;

(e) by fax (6PD3).

Parties can also agree service by other means (rule 6.8).

6.2   Personal service (rule 6.4)

(a) On individuals, by leaving the document with that individual.

(b) On companies or other corporations, by leaving the document with a person holding a 'senior position', as defined by the Practice Direction, within the company or corporation.

(c) On a partnership, provided that partnerships are being sued in the name of their firm, by leaving it with any of the partners, or else, on a person having at the time of service 'the control or management of the partnership business at the principal place of business' of the partnership.

6.3   Service by the court

As provided in rule 6.3(1), documents issued or prepared by the court are served by the court; but this is subject to exceptions. Namely, r 6.3(1) does not apply wherever:

- a rule provides that a party themselves must serve;
- the party on whose behalf the document is to be served informs the court, in writing, that they wish to serve themselves;
- the court itself orders otherwise;
- the court has sent a notice of non-service;
- there is a Practice Direction.

Service will normally be by first class post (6PD8.1).

6.4   Service on companies

Whilst the Rules (rule 6.4(4)) provide that service on a company may be by leaving it with the person holding 'a senior position' within the company or corporation, the existing rules in the Companies Act 1985 remain intact, so that, as an alternative, service may be made by leaving the document at, or posting it to, an 'authorised place', pursuant to s 725 of the Act; s 694A (service of documents on companies incorporated outside the UK and Gibraltar and having a branch in Great Britain) and s 695 (see, also, 6PD6).

Similar provisions apply to corporations, service to be wherever the corporation carries on its activities or has its principal office.

6.5 Address for service (rule 6.5)

Documents to be served outside the jurisdiction are not dealt with in the Civil Procedure Rules but continue to be governed by RSC Ord 11.

A party must give an address for service within England and Wales. If he is represented, his address for service is his solicitor's address (except, usually, in relation to service of a claim form – see below, 6.7.3). If not, he must give his residence or place of business (unless he does not reside or carry on business in England and Wales, in which case he may give any address within England and Wales – rule 6.5(3)). Note, however, that, for the purposes of automatic transfer, the 'defendant's home court' excludes the court for the area where the defendant's solicitors are, unless it happens to be the same as the defendant's home or trading address.

If an unrepresented party has not given an address for service, the document must be sent as follows (rule 6.5(6)):

- Individual:
  o usual or last known residence.
- Proprietor of a business:
  o usual or last known residence; or
  o place of business or last known place of business.
- Individual suing or sued in name of firm (see, also, 6PD4):
  o usual or last known residence; or
  o principal or last known place of business.
- Corporation incorporated in England and Wales (other than a company):
  o principal office; or
  o any place within the jurisdiction where it carries on its activities and which has a real connection with the claim.
- Company registered in England and Wales:
  o principal office;
  o any place of business of the company within the jurisdiction which has a real connection with the claim.
- Any other company or corporation:
  o any place within the jurisdiction where the corporation carries on its activities;
  o any place of business of the company within the jurisdiction.

6.6   Deemed service (rule 6.7)

6.6.1   First class post

Deemed effective the second day after the document was posted to the address for service (see below) of the person to be served.

6.6.2   Leaving the document

Deemed effective the day *after* the document was left at the address for service (see below, 6.7.3) of the person to be served.

6.6.3   Through a document exchange (6PD2)

Deemed effective the second day after it was left at the document exchange. The address for service of the party to be served must include a document exchange box number or his writing paper, or that of his solicitor must set one out. This method of service cannot be used if the party has indicated in writing that he is unwilling to be served by it.

6.6.4   By fax (6PD3)

Deemed effective on the day of transmission if transmitted before 4 pm on a business day (or the next business day if transmitted otherwise) to a fax number indicated in writing for the purpose by the party to be served or his solicitor. A fax number set out on solicitors' writing paper is assumed to be so indicated, as is one set out on a statement of case or a response to a claim filed with the court.

6.6.5   By other electronic means

Permitted only when both the party serving and the party to be served are legally represented, and the latter's solicitors have agreed in writing to the method of service and have provided an email address or other electronic identification. Effective the second day after the day on which it was transmitted.

6.6.6   Service out of business hours

When documents are served after 5 pm on a business day, or on the weekend or a Bank Holiday, the document shall be deemed as having been served on the next business day (rule 6.7(2)).

6.7 Service of the claim form

The general rule is that the claim form must be served on the defendant within four months from issue (six months where service is out of the jurisdiction (rule 7.5)). An order may be made extending time (rule 7.6), the application to be supported by evidence.

6.7.1 Proof of service

A rule, Practice Direction or order may require a certificate of service to be filed (see below, 6.7.4).

6.7.2 Non-service by court (rule 6.11)

The court will only try to effect service at the address initially given by the claimant. Where this fails, the court will give notice to that effect. It then becomes the party's responsibility to effect service (6PD8.2).

6.7.3 Address for service of claim form (rule 6.13)

The defendant's address for service must be given in the claim form if he is to be served by the court. His solicitor's address should be given as his address for service only if the solicitor is authorised to accept service. When a claim form is or particulars of claim are served on a partner or person having control or management of a partnership business at its principal place of business, notice must also be served as to the capacity in which the person is served. If the court effects service, it will provide a notice to this effect. If the party effects service, he must file a certificate of service within seven days.

6.7.4 Certificate of service (rule 6.10)

A certificate of service must state that a document has not been returned undelivered and, where the method of service was:

- by post, the date of posting;
- personal, the date of personal service;
- through a document exchange, the date of delivery to it;
- by delivery to or leaving at a permitted place, the date of delivery or leaving;
- by fax, the date and time of transmission;

- by other electronic means, the date of transmission and details of the means of transmission;
- by alternative method permitted by the court, the details required by the court.

Where a contract makes provision for service and the claim is in respect only of that contract, it may be served in accordance with that provision (rule 6.15). The court may, in some circumstances, by order authorise service on the agent of a defendant who is abroad (rule 6.16). The application must be supported by evidence and may be made without notice.

6.7.5 Service personnel

Guidance notes as to service on members of HM Forces and members of the US Air Force are annexed to the Practice Direction to Part 6.

6.8   Children and patients (rule 6.6)

The person who must be served with the claim form where the child is not also a patient, is the child's parent or guardian, or, if there is none, the person with whom the child resides or in whose care he is. Claim forms where the person to be served is a 'patient' is – or, if there is one – the person authorised under Part VII of the Mental Health Act 1983 to conduct proceedings in the name of the patient – or the person with whom the patient resides, or in whose care the patient is. With regard to any other document, after the claim form, service will be on the 'litigation friend'.

7 Responses to Claim

7.1 General

A copy of the particulars of claim, or the claim form if it contains the particulars of claim, is sent to the defendants, accompanied by a 'response pack' (rule 7.8(1)).

The pack includes:

- an admission form (N9A);
- a defence and counterclaim form (N90) (a copy of this is set out below, Chapter 24);
- an acknowledgment of service (N9).

7.2 Options for the defendant

To complete:

(a) the admission form if the claim, or the amount claimed, is admitted; or

(b) the admission form and the defence form, if part claim is admitted (see below); or

(c) the defence form if the whole claim is disputed or a claim is made against the claimant; or

(d) the acknowledgment of service where the defendant needs 28 days rather than 14 to prepare his defence or where he contests the court's jurisdiction (rule 10.1(3) and see rule 11 generally).

7.3 The acknowledgment of service

Acknowledgments of service are to be filed within 14 days after the date of service of the particulars of claim, or within 14 days of the date of service of the claim form if it contains the particulars of claim (rule 10.3(1)). The above time limit will not apply where different and longer periods are specified for claim forms served out of the jurisdiction (rule 10.3(2)).

The court informs claimants of receipt of an acknowledgment of service, which itself has to provide an address to which documents for the defendant are to be sent.

7.4   Default judgments

A default judgment may be entered whenever a defendant fails to file an acknowledgment of service within the specified period or does not, within that period, file a defence (see below) or serve an admission (rule 12.1). However, where the claim form states that particulars of claim are to follow, the defendant need not respond until the particulars of claim have been served upon him.

Default judgment may not be entered in the following cases (rule 12.2):

- those for delivery of goods under the Consumer Credit Act 1974;
- where the Part 8 procedure (see above, Chapter 5) is used (but see below);
- by the claimant, where the defendant has applied for summary judgment;
- In Part 20 claims (see below, Chapter 8) other than counterclaims, that is, default judgment does apply to counterclaims but not to others;
- where a Practice Direction so provides.

Where Part 8 procedure is being used, if the defendant fails to file an acknowledgment, he will be unable to take any active part in the hearing without the leave of the court (rule 8.4) (see above, Chapter 5).

7.4.1 Counterclaims

Where there is a Part 20 claim, a default judgment can now be obtained in the county court on a counterclaim. If the counterclaim is for money or delivery of goods where the defendant to the counterclaim is given the alternative of paying the value of the goods, this can be done administratively.

7.4.2 Other Part 20 claims

Except for contribution or indemnity between defendants to the claim (where a default judgment cannot be obtained), special rules apply where the Part 20 defendant has failed to file an acknowledgment or defence. In such cases:

- the defendant is deemed to admit the Part 20 claim;
- the defendant is bound by any judgment in the main proceedings so far as it is relevant to the Part 20 claim;
- the claimant may obtain judgment by filing a request in the relevant practice form, provided that:
  - o default judgment has been taken against that Part 20 claimant, and
  - o he has satisfied that default judgment, and
  - o the remedy he seeks is limited to contribution or indemnity.

If any of these conditions is not met, the Part 20 claimant may only enter default judgment if he obtains the court's permission.

7.4.3 Obtaining a default judgment

There are two mechanisms in place for obtaining default judgments, depending on the nature of the claim:

(a) A request for judgment under Part 12 is available for money claims (rule 12.4(1)). A money claim will include both one for specified sums, and one which is in respect of unspecified damages. The procedure is that judgment is entered simply on filing a request for default judgment, and this, of course, is done without any consideration of the claim's merits (rule 12.4(2)).

(b) Where the claim is for a remedy other than a money claim, or is a claim only for costs other than fixed costs, and also in certain other cases which are set out in rule 12.10, an application must be made for judgment using the Part 23 application procedure (see below, Chapter 15). On such an application, a hearing will be given, and the court will give '*such judgment as it appears to the Court that the claimant is entitled to on his statement of case*' (rule 12.11(1)). Under this procedure, that is, an application for judgment, the court will consider the merits.

Most default judgments are likely to be entered simply from filing a request in the appropriate form (see below).

7.4.4 Conditions for entering judgments in default

In all cases, whether by way of a request for judgment or an application for a default judgment, the court must be satisfied that (rule 12.3 and 12PD4.1):

(a) the particulars of claim have been served – this is likely to be obvious from the certificate of service on the court file;

(c) the defendant has not filed an acknowledgment of service, or has not filed a defence, and in either case the time for doing so has expired;

(d) the defendant has not satisfied the claim;

(e) the defendant has not filed or served an admission together with a request for time to pay; and

(f) the defendant has not made an application for summary judgment which has not been disposed of.

7.4.5 Special cases requiring an application (rule 12.10)

These are:

(a) against children and patients;

(c) for costs other than fixed costs;

(d) by one spouse against the other on a claim in tort;

(e) for delivery up of goods where the defendant will not be allowed the alternative of paying their value;

(f) against the Crown;

(g) against persons or organisations who enjoy immunity from civil jurisdiction under the provisions of the International Organisations Acts 1968 and 1981.

7.4.6 Forms

For default judgments by request, use Forms N205A or N255, or, where the amount is to be decided by the court, Form N225B (see below, Chapter 24).

7.5   Admissions (Part 14)

See rule 14.1:

(1) A party may admit the truth of the whole or any part of another party's case.

(2) He may do this by giving notice in writing (such as in a statement of case or by letter).

(3) Where the only remedy which the claimant is seeking is the payment of money, the defendant may also make an admission in accordance with –

    (a) rule 14.4 (admission of whole claim for specified amount of money);

    (b) rule 14.5 (admission of part of claim for specified amount of money);

    (c) rule 14.6 (admission of liability to pay whole of claim for unspecified amount of money); or

    (d) rule 14.7 (admission of liability to pay claim for unspecified amount of money where defendant offers a sum in satisfaction of the claim).

7.5.1 Admission of whole of claim for specified sum

In this case, the defendant must serve the admission direct on the claimant. The claimant then files it with his request for judgment, using Form 205A (rule 14.4(4)).

7.5.2 Admission of part of claim for specified sum

The defendant files the admission with the court, which then serves a copy on the claimant. The claimant has 14 days in which to notify the court as to whether he accepts the offer or not (rule 14.5(3)–(5)). If he does not do so, the claim is stayed until the claimant notifies. If the defendant accepts the offer, he obtains judgment by filing a request, but if he does not, then the claim is treated as defended (rule 26.3(4)(a)).

7.5.3 Admission of claim for unspecified sum

The admission is filed in court and the court serves a copy on the claimant. The claimant has 14 days to respond (by filing a request for judgment), or the claim is stayed until he does so (rule 14.6(1)–(5)). When the claimant files the request for judgment, judgment is entered 'for an amount to be determined by the court', and the file is referred to the judge for him to give management directions (rules 14.6(7) and 14.8).

7.5.4 Admission of claim for unspecified sum coupled with offer in satisfaction

Where such an admission is made, it is filed in court and the court serves a copy on the claimant, who has 14 days to respond (rule 14.7(2)–(3)). If he does not respond, the claim is stayed until he does so. If the claimant accepts the offer, he may obtain judgment for the amount offered by filing a request (rule 14.7(4)).

7.5.5 Requests for time to pay

If a defendant makes an admission under rules 14.4, 14.5 or 14.7, he may request time to pay (rule 14.9(1)–(6)). The claimant may agree the request or reject it. If he rejects it, the court will determine the time or rate of payment (rule 14.10(4)).

7.6   Contents of defence

7.6.1 Address for service

The defence form provides a space for address for service. This must be within the jurisdiction and will be that of the legal representative, if he has signed the acknowledgment of service (rule 10.5).

In response, a 'defence' must (rule 16.5):

(a) State:
  (i)   which parts of the claim the defendant admits;
  (ii) which parts he denies;
  (iii) which parts he neither admits nor denies, because he does not know whether they are true, but which he wishes the claimant to prove;

(b) give the defendant's version of the facts in so far as they differ from those in the statement of claim;

(c) say why the defendant disputes the claimant's entitlement to any, or to a particular, remedy or the value of the claim or assessment of damages; and

(d) specify any document vital to the defence.

7.6.2 Practical implications

As with particulars of claim, defences must now be much more specific and must answer the claim. Thus, a bare denial, such as 'the defendant denies the claim and puts the claimant to strict proof', will no longer be acceptable and is likely to be struck out. The same is true of a 'holding defence', such as 'the defendant denies the claim and will be filing a full defence in due course'. In the case of road traffic accidents, the defendant will be expected to give their version of the accident.

Damages can be admitted, if desired for the purpose of the action whichever way it goes, but otherwise a defendant shall not be taken to admit damages, unless he does expressly admit them.

Statements of value (see above, Chapter 4) can be disputed, in which case the defendant must say why and, if able, give his own statement (rule 16(6)). Representative capacities must be stated in a defence and, if an acknowledgment of service has not been given, an address for service must be supplied (rule 16(7) and (8)).

7.6.3 Verification of truth

Part 22 requires a defence to be verified by a statement of truth (15PD2.1) (as it is a 'statement of case' – see above, Chapter 4). The form of the statement of truth is as follows (15PD2.2): '[I believe][the defendant believes] that the facts stated in this defence are true.'

The statement of truth is in fact printed on the Form N90, above the space for signatures.

Note 10PD4:

4.2 Where the defendant is a company or other corporation, a person holding a senior position in the company or corporation may sign the acknowledgment of service on the defendant's behalf, but must state the position he holds.

4.3 Each of the following persons is a person holding a senior position:

1   in respect of a registered company or corporation, a director, the treasurer, secretary, chief executive, manager or other officer of the company or corporation, and

2   in respect of a corporation which is not a registered company, in addition to those persons set out in (1), the mayor, chairman, president, town clerk or similar officer of the corporation.

4.4 Where the defendant is a partnership, the acknowledgment of service may be signed by:

1   any of the partners, or

2   a person having the control or management of the partnership business.

4.5 Children and patients may acknowledge service only by their litigation friend or his legal representative unless the court otherwise orders

7.6.4 Defence: details

Under rule 16.5, a defendant who:

(3) (a) fails to deal with an allegation; and

(b) has set out in his defence the nature of his case in relation to the issue to which that allegation is relevant, shall be taken to require that allegation to be proved.

(4) Where the claim includes a money claim, a defendant shall be taken to require that any allegation relating to the amount of money claimed be proved unless he expressly admits the allegation.

(5) Subject to paragraphs (3) and (4), a defendant who fails to deal with an allegation shall be taken to admit that allegation.

(6) If the Defendant disputes the claimant's statement of value under rule 16.3 (*in relation to a claim for personal injuries*) he must:

(a)   state why he disputes it; and

(b)   if he is able, give his own statement of the value of the claim.

In personal injury cases, additional provisions are required by 16PD15:

15.1   Where the claim is for personal injuries and the claimant has attached a medical report in respect of his alleged injuries, the defendant should:

(1) state in his defence whether he

(a) agrees,

(b) disputes, or

(c) neither agrees nor disputes but has no knowledge of the matters contained in the medical report,

(2) where he disputes any part of the medical report, give in his defence his reasons for doing so, and

(3) where he has obtained his own medical report on which he intends to rely, attach it to his defence.

15.2   Where the claim is for personal injuries and the claimant has included a schedule of past and future expenses and losses, the defendant should include in or attach to his defence a counter-schedule stating:

(1) which of those items he

(a) agrees,

(b) disputes, or

(c) neither agrees nor disputes but has no knowledge of, and

(2) where any items are disputed, supplying alternative figures where appropriate.

For special requirements for defences in defamation cases, see 16PD16.

7.6.5 Time for filing defence

The period for filing a defence is 14 days after service of the particulars of claim, or 28 days after service where the defendant has filed an acknowledgement of service (rule 15(4)(1)). These periods will not apply where different and longer periods are specified where claim forms are served out of the jurisdiction; nor where the defendant has made an Application disputing the court's jurisdiction; nor in those cases where the claimant has applied for summary judgment before a defence has been filed, in which case the defendant need not file his defence until the summary judgment hearing (rule 15.4(2)) (see below, Chapter 9).

7.6.6 Extension by agreement

The parties can agree for an extension, but not beyond 28 days further and beyond what is specified in the rules (rule 15.5(1)). Both parties must, in such cases, notify the court of the agreed extension (rule 5.5(2)).

7.6.7   Service

The same rules apply as with any other document, namely, that they will be served by the court, save where a rule says otherwise or a party wishes to serve himself and so notifies the court, or where there is a Practice Direction as to service, or the court otherwise orders, or those cases in which a notice of non-service has been sent out by the court (rule 6(2)) (see above, Chapter 6).

7.6.8   Defence of set-off

Rule 16.6:

> Where a defendant –
>
> (a) contends he is entitled to money from the claimant; and
>
> (b) relies on this as a defence to the whole of part of the claim,
>
> the contention may be included in the defence and set off against the claim.

7.6.9   Defence of payment in money claims (rule 15.10)

If this is the defence, to shorten matters, the claimant will receive a Notice from the court asking him, the complainant, to state whether he wishes to proceed, and if he does so, send a copy of that response to the defendant; the proceedings will be stayed in any event within 28 days after service of the court's notice, if the claimant fails at all to respond to it; application can then be made by any party to restore.

7.6.10 Stay of proceedings where six months has elapsed (rule 15.11)

Where six months have expired since the end of the period for filing a defence, and neither a defence, an admission or a counterclaim has been filed, nor an admittance, and the claimant has not entered or applied for judgment, then the claim is automatically stayed; parties may apply for the stay to be lifted.

7.7 Reply (rule 16.7)

A reply, as before the county court, is optional; if the claimant does wish to file a reply in response to the defence, he should do so when he files his allocation questionnaire. There are to be no further 'statements of case' after a reply without the permission of the court (rule 15.9).

See rule 16.7:

(1) A Claimant who does not file a reply to the defence shall not be taken to admit the matters raised in the defence.

(2) A claimant who:

    (a) files a reply to a defence, but

    (b) fails to deal with a matter raised in the defence, shall be taken to require that matter to be proved.

8 Part 20 Claims

8.1 General

Any claim, other than a claim by a claimant against a defendant, is called a 'Part 20 Claim'. The old reference to 'third party' has gone.

Part 20 claims fall into four categories:

(a) counterclaims against claimant(s);

(b) counterclaims against claimant(s) and a non-party;

(c) claims for contribution or indemnity made between defendants to the claim;

(d) any other claim made by a defendant against a non-party.

Any person who becomes a defendant to a Part 20 claim may himself bring a similar claim against another (whether or not already a party), and this, too, will be a Part 20 claim.

8.2 Procedure Rules

See 20PD3:

The Civil Procedure Rules apply generally to Part 20 Claims as if they were claims. However, by Rule 20.2, the following Rules do NOT apply to Part 20 Claims:

(a) Rules 7.5 and 7.6 (time within which a claim form may be served);

(b) Rule 16.3(5) (statement of value where claim to be issued in the High Court); and

(c) Part 26 (case management – preliminary stage).

And, by rule 20.3:

(a) Part 12 (default judgment); and

(b) Part 14 (admissions) except Rules 14.1(1) and (2) (which provide that a party may admit in writing the truth of another party's case) and 14.3 (admission by notice in writing – application for judgment).

8.3   Counterclaims (rules 20.4(2) and 20.5(1), (2) and (3))

A counterclaim may be made without permission where:

- it is brought against the claimant or, if there are several claimants, one or more of them; and
- it is filed with the defence.

Thus, leave will be required to commence a counterclaim:

- before or after filing of the counterclaimant's defence;
- where no defence is filed.

8.3.1 Form of counterclaim and the reply

See 20PD6.1 and 6.2:

1   Where a defendant to a claim serves A COUNTERCLAIM under this Part, the defence and counterclaim should normally form one document with the counterclaim following on from the defence.

2   Where a claimant serves A REPLY and a defence to counterclaim, the reply and the defence to counterclaim should normally form one document with the defence to counterclaim following on from the reply.

A blank form for a Part 20 claim is part of 'the response pack' sent to the defendant by the court with the claim form.

Note rule 4(1), (2) and (3):

4.1 The contents of a Part 20 claim should be verified by a STATEMENT OF TRUTH. Part 22 requires a statement of case to be verified by a statement of truth.

4.2 The form of the statement of truth should be as follows:

'[I believe][Part 20 claimant believes] that the facts stated in this statement of case are true.'

4.3 Attention is drawn to rule 32.14 which sets out the consequences of verifying a statement of case containing a false statement without an honest belief in its truth.

8.3.2 Filing and service

The counterclaim is made by filing particulars of the counterclaim and must be served with the defence. Time for defence to counterclaim is 14 days. Acknowledgement of service may not be filed in relation to a counterclaim, which is anomalous because it may be used for every other form of Part 20 claim, thereby giving the defendant to the Part 20 claim an additional 14 days in which to file a defence.

A counterclaimant may thus be in the position of having to file his allocation questionnaire before he knows how the claimant (defendant to counterclaim) pleads to the counterclaim. However, rule 3.1(2) provides:

> Except where these Rules provide otherwise, the court may –
>
> (a) extend or shorten the time for compliance with any rule, practice direction or court order (even if an application for extension is made after the time for compliance has expired) ...

Rule 20.12 provides that, where a Part 20 claim form is served on a person who is not already a party, it must be accompanied by:

(a) a form for defending the claim;

(b) a form for admitting the claim;

(c) a form for acknowledging service; and

(d) a copy of:

    (i) every statement of case which has already been served in the proceedings; and

    (ii) such other documents as the court may direct.

See, also, rule 20.8:

(1) Where a part 20 claim may be made without the court's permission, the Part 20 claim form must –

    (a) in the case of a counterclaim, be served on every other party when a copy of the defence is served;

    (b) in the case of any other Part 20 claim, be served on the person against whom it is made within 14 days after the date on which the party making the Part 20 claim files his defence.

(2) Paragraph (1) does not apply to a claim for contribution or indemnity made in accordance with Rule 20.6.

(3) Where the court gives permission to make a Part 20 claim, it will at the same time give directions as to the service of the Part 20 claim.

As for the title on the claim form, see 20PD7(1)–(5).

8.4   Counterclaims against a non-party

Permission is always required to bring a new party into the proceedings and, thus, is required to make this type of Part 20 claim.

8.5   Contribution and indemnity

This type of Part 20 claim may be brought without leave at any time by a defendant who has acknowledged service or filed a defence. The claim is made by filing a notice and serving it on the defendant to the Part 20 claim. The Part 20 claim must be served within 14 days of issue. The rules about filing defence and acknowledgment of service are the same as for a claim.

See rule 20.6:

A defendant who has filed an acknowledgment of service or a defence may make a Part 20 claim for Contributions or Indemnity against another defendant by –

(a) filing a notice containing a statement of the nature and grounds of his claim; and

(b) serving that notice on the other defendant.

8.6   Other Part 20 claims

The procedure for making any other Part 20 claim brought by a defendant against any person who is not already a party for contribution or indemnity, or some other remedy (rule 20.7).

This type of Part 20 claim may be made without leave (now referred to as 'permission') where it is issued before or at the same time as the defence of the defendant making the Part 20 claim and is made by filing a Part 20 claim form. The Part 20 claim must be served within 14 days after the party making the Part 20 claim files his defence, and the rules as to acknowledgment of service and defence apply.

An application for permission to make a Part 20 claim may be made without notice. If permission is given, the judge must at the same time give directions for the filing of defence to the Part 20 claim.

8.7   Applications for permission where the counterclaim, or other Part 20 claim, is not served with the defence

See 20PD2.1:

2.1 An application for permission to make a Part 20 claim must be supported by EVIDENCE stating:

(1) the state which the action has reached;

(2) the nature of the claim to be made by the Part 20 claimant or details of the question or issue which needs to be decided;

(3) a summary of the facts on which the Part 20 Claim is based; and

(4) the name and address of the proposed Part 20 defendant.

(For further information regarding evidence see the Practice Direction which supplements Part 32.)

2.2 Where delay has been a factor contributing to the need to apply for permission to make a Part 20 claim an explanation of the delay should be given in evidence.

2.3 Where possible the applicant should provide a timetable of the action to date.

2.4 Rules 20.5(2) and 20.7(5) allow applications to be made to the court without notice unless the court otherwise directs.

Where the court gives permission to make a Part 20 claim later, after defence has been served, directions will be given as to service (rule 20.8).

8.8   Case management under Part 20 (rule 20.13)

If a defence to a Part 20 claim is filed, the case will be referred to the procedural judge to consider giving management directions. Note that Part 26 (allocation) (see below, Chapter 10) does not apply to Part 20 claims, but the judge:

• must, so far as possible, manage the Part 20 claim(s) with the claim; and

• may order that a Part 20 claim be managed separately from the claim.

For the court's powers at the case management hearing, see 20PD 5.3 and 5.4.

Rule 20.9 applies whenever the court is considering whether to permit a Part 20 claim, dismiss it, or require it to be dealt with separately.

The matters to which the court may have regard include:

(a) the connection between the Part 20 claim and the claim made by the claimant against the defendant;

(b) whether the Part 20 claimant is seeking substantially the same remedy which some other party is claiming from him; and

(c) whether the Part 20 claimant wants the court to decide any question connected with the subject matter of the proceedings:

(i) not only between existing parties but also between existing parties and a person not already a party; or

(ii) against an existing party not only in a capacity in which he is already a party but also in some further capacity.

8.9 Default judgment in Part 20 claims (rule 20.11)

Note that default judgment can now be obtained in the county court on a counterclaim. If the counterclaim is for money, or delivery of goods where the defendant (to the counterclaim) is given the alternative of paying the value of the goods, this can be done administratively.

For other types of Part 20 claim, except claims for contribution or indemnity between defendants to the claim (where a default judgment cannot be obtained at all), there are special rules where the Part 20 defendant has failed to file an acknowledgment of service or defence. In such cases, r 20.11 applies, under which:

• the defendant is deemed to admit the Part 20 claim;

• the defendant is bound by any judgment in the main proceedings so far as it is relevant to the Part 20 claim;

• the claimant may obtain judgment by filing a request in the relevant practice form, provided that:

o default judgment has been taken against that Part 20 claimant; and

o he has satisfied that default judgment; and

o the remedy he seeks is limited to contribution or indemnity.

If any of those conditions is not met, the Part 20 claimant may only enter default judgment if he obtains the court's permission.

8.10 Practical implications

There is no doubt that the 'lumping in' of counterclaims with third party and similar claims under the umbrella of 'Part 20 claims' is probably only likely to cause confusion. Thus, a defendant who counterclaims becomes also a 'Part 20 claimant' while a claimant becomes, in addition, a 'Part 20 defendant'!

It is also important to note the occasions when permission is required to issue a Part 20 claim as, basically, permission will always be required unless the Part 20 claim accompanies the defence.

Note that a court fee is payable on a counterclaim in the same way as a claim. The court officers have little difficulty with insisting upon this if the counterclaim is filed with the defence, but it must also be remembered that the fee must also be paid if the counterclaim is filed, with permission, at some later stage. Failure to pay the fee may result in the court refusing to consider the counterclaim.

Although a 'response pack' is provided to defendants (see above, Chapter 7), no such 'pack' is given to defendants to a counterclaim (that is, original claimants), who must file a defence within the time limits in order to avoid a default judgment. This may lead to some claimants not knowing what to do when they are served with a counterclaim.

9 Summary Judgment and Disposal

9.1 Summary judgment (Part 24)

9.1.1 General

Part 24 makes broad provision for deciding claims or issues without a trial, replaces the old RSC Ord 14 and CCR Ord 9 r 14 and is available to both claimants and defendants. The court can also grant summary judgment of its own initiative (see below). Except with permission, claimants must wait until a defendant has filed an acknowledgment of service or a defence before applying for summary judgment (rule 24.4(1)). If a defendant does neither, then a claimant can proceed by way of a default judgment (see above, Chapter 7).

Where the application is made before a defence is filed, the defendant against whom it is made need not file a defence (rule 24.4(2)). However, where the defendant is seeking summary judgment against the claimant, it does not appear that the defendant is relieved from having to file a defence.

Summary judgment is now available in small claims matters, from which it was previously disallowed.

The Allocation Questionnaire asks the parties if they intend to make an application for summary judgment. The Part 24 procedure can also be used where just a point of law is involved (24PD1.3(1))

9.1.2 Proceedings excluded from Part 24

Summary judgment *cannot* be given against:

- a defendant in proceedings for possession of residential property;

- a mortgagor in mortgage possession proceedings;
- a former tenant holding over.

Nor can a summary judgment be given in proceedings for an admiralty claim *in rem*, or in contentious probate (rule 24.3). For applications against claimants, there are not any excluded proceedings (rule 24.3(1)).

Mortgages and tenancy agreements

An application can be made under Part 24 if it is a claim for specific performance of an agreement for the sale, purchase, exchange, mortgage or charge on any property, or for the grant or assignment of a lease or tenancy. Similarly, there may be an application for rescission of such an agreement, or for the forfeiture or return of any deposit made under such agreement. The application notice, evidence in support, and a draft order must be served no less than four clear days before the hearing of any such Application (24PD7).

9.1.3 Claims for an order for accounts and inquiries

Whenever the claim form expressly or by implication involves accounts and inquiries, an application may be made under Part 24 for a summary order so directing (24PD6).

9.1.4 Procedure

The application

The court is expressly empowered to fix a summary judgment hearing of its own initiative (rule 24.4(3)), particularly to further the 'objective' of deciding which issues need investigation and which can be dealt with summarily. In addition, on allocation, or possibly earlier, the court will always consider its powers under rule 3.4(1) to consider sanctions or summary disposal (see below, summary disposal).

Where the court is considering making an order for summary judgment of its own initiative, it must give each party likely to be affected by the order at least three days' notice of the hearing (rule 3.3 (3)). However, this seems to conflict with rule 24.4(3), which states that the respondent is entitled to at least 14 days' notice of the date of the hearing and of the issues to be decided. It would appear, therefore, that the effect of rule 24.4 is to extend the period provided for in rule 3.3(3).

Applications by a party under Part 24 may be based on a point of law, the evidence which can reasonably be expected, or lack of it, or a combination of both (rule 24.2).

No particular form is prescribed, but Form N244 may be used (see Part 23 and below, Chapter 15). It must contain a statement that it is an application for summary judgment (24PD2(2)), identify concisely the point of law or provision in a document on which the applicant relies, and/or state that the applicant believes that the respondent has no real prospect of succeeding and that there is no other reason why the matter should go to trial (242(3)). Non-compliance with these technicalities is likely to be fatal to the application (see *Barclays Bank v Piper* (1995) *The Times*, 31 May).

The application notice should draw the attention of the respondent to rule 24.5(1) (24PD2(5)), that is:

(1) If the respondent to an application for summary judgment wishes to rely on written evidence at the hearing, he must:

   (a) file the written evidence; and

   (b) serve copies on every other party to the application,

   at least 7 days before the summary judgment hearing.

The respondent is entitled to 14 days' notice of the application, setting out the issues that the court has to decide (rule 24.4(3)). Notice must be given, either by the party who brings the application or by the court if the hearing is fixed of the court's own motion.

The hearing

Witness statements (see below, Chapter 17) may be used at the hearing of the application, but there is no requirement for them (because the statement of case and/or application notice when verified by the statement of truth can stand as evidence).

The application will normally be heard by a district judge or master (24PD3.1), although either of them could direct that it is heard by a circuit judge (24PD3.2).

The principles

A case that is merely 'arguable', as under the old rules, will not suffice now to resist applications if (rule 24.2):

(a) [the Court] considers –

    (i) that the claimant has no real prospect of succeeding on the claim or issue; or

    (ii) that the defendant has no real prospect of successfully defending the claim or issue; and

(b) there is no other *compelling* reason why the case or issue should be disposed of at a trial.

In an application for summary judgment against a claimant under rule 24.2, the correct test is not whether the claim is bound to fail but whether the claimant has no real prospect of succeeding on the claim or issue (*Peter Robert Krafft v Camden LBC* (2000) unreported, 24 October, CA).

The test is extended to claims, replacing applications to strike out statements of case for disclosing no reasonable grounds as an alternative or in addition to making an application for summary disposal (see rule 3.4 and below). Indeed, this can be implied by the reference to rule 3.4 and it would be sensible for practitioners to consider including an application under Part 24 as an alternative to an application under rule 3.4.

Part 24 throws no burden onto the respondent to show that he has a defence or a claim, as the case may be – cf RSC Ord 14 rr 3(1) and 4(1). The burden of proving that the other side does not have a claim or defence is on the applicant.

9.1.5 Conditional orders (24PD4.3)

Where it appears to the court that it is possible that a claim or defence may succeed but improbable that it will do so, it may make a conditional order. A conditional order may require a party to pay into court and/or take some further step in the action against the sanction of dismissal or strike out; at the same time, further directions are likely to be made (rule 24 PD 5(1)).

Rule 3.1(5) provides:

(5) The court may order a party to pay a sum of money into court.

(6) When exercising its power under paragraph (5) the court must have regard to –

(a) the amount in dispute; and

(b) the costs which the parties have incurred or which they may incur.

See, also, rule 37.2:

(1) This rule applies where the court makes an order permitting a defendant to defend or to continue to defend on condition that he makes a payment into court.

(2) Where a defendant to a money claim makes such a payment into court he may choose to treat the whole or any part of the money paid into court as a Part 36 payment.

9.1.6 Final orders

Subject to the question of conditional orders (see above), final orders may be:

- judgment on the claim;
- striking out, or dismissal of claim;
- application dismissed.

If the claim proceeds, directions will be given, as on a case management conference.

Fixed costs may be awarded on an application for summary judgment (rule 45.1(2)). This will be dependent on the amount awarded. For details, see rule 45.4 of Table 2.

9.1.7 Practical implications

In the light of the more reasonable test for summary judgment, practitioners are advised that it might be worthwhile considering making such applications.

9.2 Summary disposal (rule 1.4(2)(c), 3PD1.1)

9.2.1 General

Rule 1.4(2)(b) includes as an example of active case management the summary disposal of issues which do not need full investigation at a trial. The rules give distinct powers which may be used to achieve this. Rule 3.4 provides:

(1) In this rule and rule 3.5, reference to a statement of case includes reference to part of a statement of case.

(2) The court may strike out a statement of case if it appears to the court –

(a) that the statement of case discloses no reasonable grounds for bringing or defending the claim;

(b) that the statement of case is an abuse of the court's process or is otherwise likely to obstruct the just disposal of the proceedings; or

(c) that there has been a failure to comply with a rule, practice direction or court order.

The Practice Direction (rule 3.4PD1.4) gives examples of the type of claim that should be struck out:

(1) those which set out no facts indicating what the claim is about, for example 'Money owed £5000',

(2) those which are incoherent and make no sense,

(3) those which contain a coherent set of facts but those facts, even if true, do not disclose any legally recognisable claim against the defendant.

This includes claims which are 'vexatious, scurrilous or obviously ill-founded'. As far as defences are concerned, included in those that should be considered for strike out is a defence if (3.4PD1.6):

(1) it consists of a bare denial or otherwise sets out no coherent statement of facts, or

(2) the facts it sets out, while coherent, would not even if true amount in law to a defence to the claim.

A court officer has power to refer a claim or defence to a judge at any time if he considers that it may fall within the above criteria (rule 3.4, PD 2/3).

Note, also, rule 3.4(4):

Where:

(a) the court has struck out a claimant's statement of case;

(b) the claimant has been ordered to pay costs to the defendant; and

(c) before the claimant pays those costs, he starts another claim against the same defendant, arising out of facts which are the same or substantially the same as those relating to the claim in which the statement of case was struck out,

the court may, on the application of the defendant, *stay* that other claim until the costs of the first claim have been paid.

9.2.2 Relief from sanctions

See below, 10.7.1.

10 Case Management by the Court

10.1 General

The court's duty to manage cases is set out at rule 1.4, which can be found above (see 1.6). This is expanded upon by rule 3.1(2):

Except where these Rules provide otherwise, the court may –

(a) extend or shorten the time for compliance with any rule, practice direction or court order (even if an application for extension is made after the time for compliance has expired);

(b) adjourn or bring forward a hearing;

(c) require a party or a party's legal representative to attend the court;

(d) hold a hearing and receive evidence by telephone or by using any other method of direct oral communication;

(e) direct that part of any proceedings (such as a counterclaim) be dealt with as separate proceedings;

(f) stay the whole or part of any proceedings or judgment either generally or until a specified date or event;

(g) consolidate proceedings;

(h) try two or more claims on the same occasion;

(i) direct a separate trial of any issue;

(j) decide the order in which issues are to be tried;

(k) exclude an issue from consideration;

(l) dismiss or give judgment on a claim after a decision on a preliminary issue;

(m) take any other step or make any other order for the purpose of managing the case and furthering the overriding objective.

10.2   Automatic transfer (rule 26.2)

Where:

- the claim is for a specified sum of money; and
- the claim was commenced in a court which is not the defendant's home court; and
- the defendant is an individual,

the claim will be automatically transferred to the defendant's home court, unless:

- the claim was commenced in a specialist list (Part 49); or
- the claim has already been transferred to the home court of another defendant under rule 13.4 (application to set judgment aside) or 14.12 (admission – determination of rate of payment); or
- rule 15.10 ('states paid' defence) or 14.5 (part admission of claim for specified sum) applies,

in which case the transfer will not take place until the claimant responds to the notice from the court as to whether he wishes the claim to proceed.

Where there is more than one defendant, the home court of the defendant who filed his defence first will determine whether, and if so to which home court, the case will be transferred.

The definition of a 'defendant's home court' is the county court for the district in which the defendant resides or carries on business, or the equivalent district registry, or the Royal Courts of Justice if it is a High Court matter (rule 2.3(1)). The previous provision whereby the 'defendant's home court' could also include the address of the defendant's solicitor has now been removed, as in many cases the solicitor was situated nowhere near his client.

10.3   Monitoring 'milestone' dates

The court is now required to specifically monitor certain important, or 'milestone', dates and take action if requirements of the court have not been complied with by those dates.

The dates are the dates for return of the allocation questionnaire (see below) and the listing questionnaire (see below, Chapter 12). The court is assisted by a computerised diary system, which produces a daily report of cases where the milestone dates have occurred, following which the file can be placed before the judge to decide what action may be necessary.

Where the court has ordered a stay for settlement (see below, 10.4.1), the file will be put before the judge after the period of stay has expired.

10.4   Allocation (Part 26)

On filing of defence, or, in the case of multiple defendants, where at least one defence has been filed and the time for filing the other defences has expired, the court will issue allocation questionnaires to all parties.

10.4.1   Allocation questionnaire (rule 26.5)

A copy of this form is provided below, Chapter 24. This is a comprehensive document requiring detailed information concerning the case. The first part of the form deals with the possibility of settlement; the second part invites representations as to track; the third part deals with pre-action protocols; the fourth part covers applications, the fifth part deals with witnesses; the sixth part covers experts; the seventh part covers location of trial; and the last parts deal with representation and estimates of length of hearing, costs and other information.

The questionnaire must be filed no later than the date specified in it, which shall be at least 14 days after the date when it is deemed served on the party in question (rule 26.4 (6)). Failure by any party to respond to the questionnaire will result in the papers being put before the court. PD2.5 suggests that, if neither side file the questionnaire, the court may make an order requiring return of the questionnaire within three days of service of the order, in default of which the court may strike out the claim or counterclaim, but, if only one side fails to return the questionnaire, the court should either allocate or fix an allocation hearing.

Where all parties request a stay to explore settlement (rule 1.4(2)(e)), or the court considers that such a stay would be desirable – one of parties having requested it – the court will direct that the proceedings be stayed for a month (rule 26.5 (2)). This date may be extended. The claimant must tell the court if settlement has been reached, in default of which the court will proceed as if it had not (rule 26.5 (5)).

10.4.2   Practical implications

Many courts have been sending out 'unless' orders where they have received no response from either of the parties after the expiry of the stay. Where both parties have indicated a desire for a stay, one will automatically be granted. However, where the request comes from just one of the parties, it will depend on whether it is the claimant, when the request is likely to be favourably considered, or from the defendant, where a circumspect view may be taken as to whether the request is merely a delaying tactic.

When every defendant has filed a questionnaire, or the time for doing so has expired (whichever is the sooner), and there is no stay for settlement (see above), the court will consider whether to allocate to track or request further information, either in writing or at an allocation hearing. Depending on the responses, the court may decide to allocate the case to one of three 'tracks'.

10.4.3 The tracks (rule 26.6)

Rule 26.6 provides:

(1) Subject to paragraphs (2) and (3) , the small claims track is the normal track for any claim which has a financial value of not more than £5,000.

(2) The small claims track is the normal track for –

    (a) any claim for personal injuries where –

        (i) the financial value of the claim is not more than £5,000; and

        (ii) the financial value of any claim for damages for personal injuries is not more than £1,000;

    (b) any claim which includes a claim by a tenant of residential premises against his landlord where –

        (i) the tenant is seeking an order requiring the landlord to carry out repairs or other work to the premises (whether or not the tenant is also seeking some other remedy);

        (ii) the cost of the repairs or other work to the premises is estimated to be not more than £1,000; and

        (iii) the financial value of any other claim for damages is not more than 1,000.

(Rule 2.3 defines 'claim for personal injuries' as proceedings in which there is a claim for damages in respect of personal injuries to the claimant or any other person or in respect of a person's death.)

(3) For the purposes of paragraph (2) 'damages for personal injuries' means damages claimed as compensation for pain, suffering, and loss of amenity and does not include any other damages which are claimed.

(4) The small claims track is not the normal track for a claim which includes a claim by a tenant of residential premises against his landlord for damages for harassment or unlawful eviction.

(5) Subject to paragraph (6), the fast track is the normal track for any claim –

(a) for which the small claims track is not the normal track; and

(b) which has a financial value of not more than £15,000.

(6) The fast track is the normal track for the claims referred to in paragraph (5) only if the court considers that –

(a) the trial is likely to last for no longer than one day; and

(b) oral expert evidence at trial will be limited to –

(i) one expert per party in relation to any expert field; and

(ii) expert evidence in two expert fields.

(7) The multi-track is the normal track for any claim for which the small claims track or the fast track is not the normal track.

10.4.4 General rules for allocation

See rule 26.7:

(1) In considering whether to allocate a claim to the normal track for that claim under rule 26.6, the court will have regard to the matters mentioned in rule 26.8(1) [see below].

(2) The court will allocate a claim which has no financial value to the track which it considers most suitable having regard to the matters mentioned in rule 26.8(1).

(3) The court will not allocate a claim to a track if the financial value of the claim, assessed by the court under rule 26.8, exceeds the limit for that track unless all the parties consent to the allocation of the claim to that track.

Claims which have no financial value will be allocated by the court to the most appropriate track, having regard to the considerations set out below (rule 26.7 (2)). Note that liability cannot be allocated to one track and quantum to another. The court does have power at any stage to reallocate a case to a different track (rule 26.10)

Rule 26.8(1) states:

When deciding the track for a claim, the matters to which the court shall have regard include –

(a) the financial value, if any, of the claim;

(b) the nature of the remedy sought;

(c) the likely complexity of the facts, law or evidence;

(d) the number of parties or likely parties;

(e) the value of any counterclaim or other Part 20 claim and the complexity of any matters relating to it;

(f) the amount of oral evidence which may be required;

(g) the importance of the claim to persons who are not parties to the proceedings;

(h) the views expressed by the parties; and

(i) the circumstances of the parties.

The court disregards any amount not in dispute and any claim for interest, costs and contributory negligence when assessing the financial value of the claim (rule 26.8(2)). For further guidance on the considerations, see 26PD7.

The parties will be served with notice of allocation, together with a copy of the allocation questionnaire served by other parties and any further information provided. Note that there is power to allocate to a track of a higher value than the claim without the consent of the parties, but not to a track of a lower value (see rule 26.7(3), above).

10.5   Allocation of possession proceedings

At the hearing of a possession case, the court may proceed to hear the case and dispose of the claim or give case management directions, including allocation to track (8PDB.13). Although rule Part 26 (allocation to track) is disapplied by Part 8.9(c), it is reapplied by PD8B.15 and Part 8.1(6)(b). Accordingly, the normal principles apply – see rule 26.6–26.10 and above.

In addition to the financial value of the claim, consideration should be given to the importance of a borrower/tenant preserving his or her home, and whether the loan was to secure a domestic or commercial loan, and the amount of the arrears. Where it is just the amount of arrears which is being challenged, there may be some argument that this may conveniently be resolved in the small claims or fast track.

There is no guidance in the Rules or any Practice Direction as to how the court should assess the financial value of defended mortgage possession claims. The same factors as in 10.4.4 above are likely to be considered.

10.6   Disposal hearings

This is the new term for assessment of damages. The procedure is to be found at para 12 of the Practice Direction to Part 26.

The need for such a hearing will arise on:

- the taking of default judgment on a claim for an unspecified sum, admission of a claim for an unspecified sum;
- the entry of judgment for an unspecified sum following an admission or order.

The procedure provides a discretionary power for the judge to allocate the assessment to a suitable track with consequent costs implications. Even if the assessment is not allocated, the judge will have to bear in mind the principle of proportionality when considering the costs to be awarded on the hearing, to ensure that the costs are reasonable in relation to the amount recovered.

Note 26PD12.8:

(1) At a disposal hearing the Court may give directions or decide the amount payable in accordance with this sub-paragraph.

(2) If the financial value of the claim (determined in accordance with Part 26) is such that the claim would, if defended, be allocated to the Small Claims Track, the Court will normally allocate it to that track and may treat the disposal hearing as a final hearing in accordance with Part 27.

(3) If the Court does not give directions and does not allocate the claim to the Small Claims Track, it may nonetheless order that the amount payable is to be decided there and then without allocating the claim to another track.

(4) Rule 32.6 applies to evidence at a disposal hearing unless the court otherwise directs.

(5) The Court will not exercise its powers under sub-para 12.8(3) unless any written evidence on which the claimant relies has been served on the defendant at least 3 days before the disposal hearing.

Note 26PD12.9 as to costs of disposal hearings:

(1) Attention is drawn to the Costs Practice Directions and in particular to the Court's power to make a summary assessment of costs.

(2) Attention is drawn to Rule 44.13(1) which provides that if an order makes no mention of costs, none are payable in respect of the proceedings to which it relates.

(3) Attention is drawn to Rule 27.14 (special rules about costs in cases allocated to the Small Claims Track).

(4) Attention is drawn to Part 45 (fixed trial costs in cases which have been allocated to the Fast Track). Part 45 will not apply to a case dealt with at a disposal hearing whatever the financial value of the claim. So the costs of a disposal hearing will be in the discretion of the Court.

Note 26PD12.10 as to the jurisdiction of masters and district judges on disposal hearings:

Unless the Court otherwise directs a Master or a District Judge may decide the amount payable under a relevant order irrespective of the financial value of the claim and of the track to which the claim may have been allocated.

10.7   Sanctions

Rule 3.1 states as follows:

(3) When the court makes an order, it may –

(a) make it subject to conditions, including a condition to pay a sum of money into court; and

(b) specify the consequence of failure to comply with the order or a condition.

(4) Where the court gives directions it may take into account whether or not a party has complied with any relevant pre-action protocol.

(5) The court may order a party to pay a sum of money into court if that party has, without good reason, failed to comply with a rule, practice direction or a relevant pre-action protocol.

(6) When exercising its power under paragraph (5) the court must have regard to –

(a) the amount in dispute; and

(b) the costs which the parties have incurred or which they may incur.

In making orders, the court does not have to wait for an application. Rule 3.3 makes it clear that it can make orders of its own initiative, subject to the right of the parties to apply to set it aside.

This power extends to striking out a statement of case (rule 3.4) (see above, Chapter 9). Sanctions are also available for non-payment of fees, and this includes striking out (rule 3.7).

10.7.1 Relief from sanctions

See Rule 3.9(1):

On an application for relief from any sanction imposed for a failure to comply with any rule, practice direction or court order the court will consider all the circumstances including –

(a) the interests of the administration of justice;

(b) whether the application for relief has been made promptly;

(c) whether the failure to comply was intentional;

(d) whether there is a good explanation for the failure;

(e) the extent to which the party in default has complied with other rules, practice directions, court orders and any relevant pre-action protocol [that is, a party can develop a record for default in the action which will mitigate against them on any further application for relief];

(f) whether the failure to comply was caused by the party or his legal representative;

(g) whether the trial date or the likely trial date can still be met if relief is granted;

(h) the effect which the failure to comply had on each party; and

(i) the effect which the granting of relief would have on each party.

(2) An application for relief must be supported by evidence.

10.7.2 Costs as a sanction

Note rule 3.8(2):

Where the sanction is the payment of costs, the party in default may only obtain relief by appealing against the order for costs.

10.7.3   Practical implications

Since the coming into force of the CPR 1998, there have been many cases concerning striking out. The conclusions that can be drawn from these cases are as follows:

- CPR principles will apply to cases commenced under the old regime;
- the court will apply the new rules without looking over its shoulder to the old regime but must concentrate on the inherent justice of a particular case in the light of the overriding objective;
- there is a wide armoury of remedies available under the new rules and striking out may not be the most appropriate remedy where some other course ought to be taken, for example, costs, limit on interest or damages;
- appeal courts will be slow to interfere with a judge's exercise of his wide discretion;
- each case will be treated on its own merits – concentrating on the intrinsic justice of a particular case in the light of the overriding objective – making a broad judgment after considering all the available possibilities. On that basis, therefore, it is likely that even recent precedents will not be of much assistance in any particular case.

10.8   Group litigation orders (GLOs)

Where there is a multi-party claim, the court may consider making a GLO (rule 19B.11(1)). This would apply where there are a large number of claimants or defendants, such as claims against tobacco companies or claims in relation to industrial diseases.

Before applying for a GLO, the applicant's solicitor should consult the Law Society's Multi-Party Action Information Service in order to obtain information about other similar cases (19BPD2.1).

The application is made in accordance with Part 23 (see below, Chapter 15), and 19BPD3.2 sets out the information required in the application. The application is made either to the High Court or to the designated civil judge (see below, Chapter 13) for the appropriate area (19BPD3). The court may consider making a GLO of its own initiative (19BPD4).

Once a GLO has been made, the court will set up a Group Register containing details of the parties (19BPD6). Any judgment or order by the court will bind all parties on the Register unless otherwise ordered (19B12).

GLOs will usually be allocated to multi-track (19BPD7(1)) and will have a 'managing judge', who will assume overall responsibility for the management of the claims (19BPD8).

Part 48 contains rules about costs where a GLO has been made.

11 Small Claims Track (Part 27)

11.1 Scope of small claims track

A claim for a remedy for harassment or unlawful eviction relating to residential premises may not be allocated to the small claims track, whatever the financial value of the claim (rule 26.7(4)).

Otherwise, the small claims track will be the normal track for:

- any claim which has a financial value of not more than £5,000 subject to the special provisions about claims for personal injuries and housing disrepair claims (rule 26.6(1));
- any claim for personal injuries which has a total financial value of not more than £5,000 where the claim for damages for personal injuries (that is, pain, suffering and loss of amenity (rule 2.3)) is not more than £1,000; and
- any claim which includes a claim by a tenant of residential premises against his landlord for repairs or other work to the premises where the estimated cost of the repairs or other work is not more than £1,000 and the financial value of any claim for damages in respect of those repairs or other work is not more than £1,000.

11.2 Exemptions from small claims track (rule 27.2)

The following rules will not apply to the small claims track:

- interim remedies, except interim injunctions (Part 25);
- disclosure and inspection (Part 31), but see below for provision of copy documents;

- evidence (Part 32) except rule 32.1 (power of court to control evidence);
- miscellaneous rules about evidence (Part 33);
- experts and assessors (Part 35) except rules 35.1 (duty to restrict expert evidence), 35.3 (experts – overriding duty to the court) and 35.8 (instructions to a single joint expert – but note that the court may order a jointly appointed expert – see 11.7 below);
- further information (Part 18) (formerly request for further and better particulars and interrogatories);
- offers to settle and payments into court (Part 36);
- hearings (Part 39) except rule 39.2 (general rule – hearing to be in public).

Note that the above rules are only disapplied *after* allocation.

11.3   Directions

At allocation stage, the procedural judge may:

- give standard directions and fix a date for the final hearing which will be set out in the notice of allocation (26PD8.2(1));
- give special directions (see *below*) in the notice and fix a date for the final hearing;
- give special directions in the notice and direct that the court will consider what further directions are to be given no later that 28 days after the date the special directions were given;
- fix a date for a preliminary hearing under rule 27.6; or
- give notice that it proposes to deal with the claim without a hearing under rule 27.10 and invite the parties to notify the court by a specified date if they agree the proposal (see below).

Standard directions are:

- a direction that each party shall, at least 14 days before the date fixed for the final hearing,, file and serve on every other party copies of all documents (including any expert's report) on which he intends to rely at the hearing; and
- any other standard directions set out in the relevant practice direction (27PD Appendix A, Form A).

Special directions are:

- directions given in addition to or instead of the standard directions (rule 27.4(1)(b)), details of which are set out in Appendix A to the

Practice Direction and include a direction to provide further information; to allow inspection of a document or object; permitting expert evidence and dealing with the instruction of the expert; requiring witness statements to be filed and served; as to the arrangements for video evidence; and that a party's statement of case be struck out if he fails to comply with a direction.

In addition, the procedural judge will have the power to order special directions tailored to the type of case (rule 27.4(1)(a)). These are set out in Appendix A to the Practice Direction (27PD2.2) and at present cover the following cases: road traffic accidents (Form B); building, vehicle repair and other similar contractual claims (Form C); return of tenancy deposits and claims for damage caused (Form D); and holiday wedding claims (Form E).

If the court gives special directions, it may (before fixing a hearing) review the position after 28 days in case further directions are needed (rule 27.4(1)(c)). The court may add to, vary or revoke directions given (rule 27.7).

The procedural judge has the power to propose that the case is dealt with on paper only, that is, without a hearing, subject to the agreement of the parties (rule 27.4(e)), although it is difficult to envisage many cases in which this will be used.

11.4   Summary judgment

Under the old rules, summary judgment was not available in small claim cases; now, rule 24.3(1) states that 'The court may give summary judgment against a claimant in any type of proceedings'. For more information, see above, Chapter 9.

11.5   Preliminary hearing

Rule 27.6(1) provides:

The court may hold a preliminary hearing for the consideration of the claim, but only –

(a) where –

(i) it considers that special directions, as defined in rule 27.4, are needed to ensure a fair hearing; and

(ii) it appears necessary for a party to attend at court to ensure that he understands what he must do to comply with the special directions; or

(b) to enable it to dispose of the claim on the basis that one or other of the parties has no real prospect of success at a final hearing; or

(c) to enable it to strike out a statement of case or part of a statement of case on the basis that the statement of case, or the part to be struck out, discloses no reasonable grounds for bringing or defending the claim.

If there is a preliminary hearing, the parties will be given at least 21 days' notice of the final hearing, unless the parties agree to a shorter period (rule 27.6 (5)).

11.6   Conduct of the hearing

Although district judges will principally be dealing with small claims track cases, there is nothing in the rules to prevent a circuit judge from hearing cases (27PD1). It will normally take place in the district judge's chambers, though it may be held in a courtroom (27PD4.2) and can be held at any place which the court considers appropriate (27PD4.1(3)). It will usually be open to the public to attend (27PD4.1(3)), but not if held away from the court or if the judge decides to hold it in private, which he may do if:

• the parties agree;

• publicity would defeat the object of the hearing;

• it involves matters relating to national security;

• it involves confidential information;

• the interests of a child or patient need to be protected; or

• the judge considers it necessary in the interests of justice (rule 39.2(3)).

The case may be presented by the parties, lawyers or lay representatives (if the party is present) on their behalf, an employee (with the court's permission) or, in the case of a company, one of the officers or employees of the company, and any other person with leave of the court (27PD3.1).

11.7   Evidence

The proceedings will be informal (rule 27.8(2)), which means that the usual rules as to evidence will not apply. See 27PD4.3:

> Rule 27.8 allows the court to adopt any method of proceeding that it considers to be fair and to limit cross-examination. The judge may in particular –

(1) ask questions of any witness himself before allowing any other person to do so,

(2) ask questions of *all* or any of the witnesses himself before allowing any other person to ask questions of any witnesses,

(3) refuse to allow cross-examination of any witness until all the witnesses have given evidence in chief,

(4) limit cross-examination of a witness to a fixed time or to a particular subject or issue, or both.

Evidence which would otherwise be inadmissible may be admitted (rule 27.8(3)). Evidence need not be on oath (rule 27.8(4)). Thus, a party may rely on a witness statement in the absence of the witness (rule 22.1.1(c)), though it must be verified by a statement of truth or it may be excluded (rule 22.3).

Expert evidence, oral or written, may not be given without permission (rule 27.5). The usual direction permitting it provides for a single expert jointly instructed (rule 35.7) (27PD Appendix A) (see below, Chapter 18).

The judge may decide to tape record the proceedings. In any event, he will be required to make a note of the central reasons for his judgment unless it is tape recorded (27PD5.4). A party will be entitled to a copy of such transcript or note of judgment on payment of the transcription charges or court fee for the note (27PD5.1 and 5.7).

11.8   Non-attendance at hearing

Non-attendance of a party may result in that party's claim or defence being struck out, unless they have previously notified the court (giving at least seven days' notice) that they will not be attending, giving reasons. In that instance, their claim or defence will be considered (rule 27.9).

Note the provisions of rule 27.9:

(1) If a party who does not attend a final hearing –

    (a) has given the court written notice at least 7 days before the date of the hearing that he will not attend; and

    (b) has, in that notice, requested the court to decide the claim in his absence,

the court will take into account that party's statement of case and any other documents he has filed when it decides the claim.

(2) If a claimant does not –

    (a) attend the hearing; and

    (b) give the notice referred to in paragraph (1),

    the court may strike out the claim.

(3) If –

    (a) a defendant does not –

        (i) attend the hearing; or

        (ii) give the notice referred to in paragraph (1); and

    (b) the claimant either –

        (i) does attend the hearing; or

        (ii) gives the notice referred to in paragraph (1),

    the court may decide the claim on the basis of the evidence of the claimant alone.

(4) If neither party attends or gives the notice referred to in paragraph (1), the court may strike out the claim and any defence and counterclaim.

In any case, the court has power to adjourn to another day and may do so if a party wishes to attend but cannot do so for good reason (27PD6.2)

11.9   Setting judgment aside for non-attendance

Application within 14 days of receipt of the judgment can be made by any party who was not present when the judgment was made (rule 27.11), unless it was granted without a hearing (see rule 27.10, above), when no application can be made (rule 27.11(5)).

The court will grant the application only if the applicant had a good reason for not attending or being represented or giving the notice, *and* has a reasonable prospect of success at the rehearing (rule 27.11(3)). If set aside, the case may be immediately heard again (rule 27.11(4)), but time and listing constraints may mitigate against this and a re-hearing may have to be ordered instead.

11.10 Appeals

As from 2 October 2000, appeals from small claims are dealt with like any other appeal from a final decision or hearing in accordance with Part 52 (see below, Chapter 22).

The grounds for appeal are as set out in Part 52 for appeals from final (as opposed to interim) orders, replacing the previous grounds of misconduct or error of law. Permission to appeal is also required. Although skeleton arguments may be of assistance, they are not compulsory in appeals against small claims decisions (r 7.7A of Part 52).

11.11 Costs

The limit on costs recoverable in small claims remains. In the small claims track, these are governed by rule 27.14, which provides:

(1) This rule applies to any case which has been allocated to the small claims track unless paragraph (5) applies.

(Rules 43.10 and 43.11 make provision in relation to orders for costs made before a claim has been allocated to the small claims track.)

(2) The court may not order a party to pay a sum to another party in respect of that other party's costs except –

    (a) the fixed costs payable under Part 44 attributable to issuing the claim;

    (b) in proceedings which included a claim for an injunction or an order for specific performance a sum not exceeding the amount specified in the relevant practice direction (£260) for legal advice and assistance relating to that claim;

    (c) costs assessed by the summary procedure in relation to an appeal under rule 27.12; and

    (d) such further costs as the court may assess by the summary procedure and order to be paid by a party who has behaved unreasonably.

(3) The court may also order a party to pay all or part of –

    (a) any court fees paid by another party;

    (b) expenses which a party or witness has reasonably incurred in travelling to and from a hearing or in staying away from home for the purposes of attending a hearing;

    (c) a sum not exceeding the amount specified in the relevant practice direction (£50) for any loss of earnings by a party or witness due to attending a hearing or to staying away from home for the purpose of attending a hearing;

    (d) a sum not exceeding the amount specified in the relevant practice direction (£200) for an expert's fees.

(4) The limits on costs imposed by this rule also apply to any fee or reward for acting on behalf of a party to the proceedings charged by a person exercising a right of audience by virtue of an order under s 11 of the Courts and Legal Services Act 1990 (a lay representative).

(5) Where –

   (a) the financial value of a claim exceeds the limit for the small claims track; but

   (b) the claim has been allocated to the small claims track in accordance with rule 26.7(3),

   the claim shall be treated, for the purposes of costs, as if it were proceeding on the fast track.

(Rule 26.7(3) allows the parties to consent to a claim being allocated to a track where the financial value of the claim exceeds the limit for that track)

11.11.1 Costs on claim reallocated from the small claims track to another track

Where a claim is allocated to the small claims track and subsequently reallocated to another track, rule 27.14 (costs on the small claims track) will cease to apply after the claim has been reallocated, and the fast track or multi-track costs rules will apply from the date of reallocation.

11.11.2 Practical implications

• Small claims to have proved a resounding success with nearly 90% of cases falling into that category. However, the increase in the jurisdiction to £5,000 has brought fairly complex cases, particularly building claims and professional negligence claims, within the small claims jurisdiction. Where that track has clearly not been appropriate, the courts have been prepared to allocate them to a higher track.

• Many small claims cases relate to technical matters outside the normal scope of the expertise of the district judge, such as dry-cleaning, repairs to vehicles or computers, building defects, etc. In those instances, the judges have been tempted to direct the appointment of a single joint expert, but it must be borne in mind that there is a limit of £200 on his fees. If the expert is unable to keep his fees within that limit, the court may have to consider reallocating the case.

- Lastly, even though the judges routinely order witness statements to be prepared, served and filed by the parties, this direction is frequently broken, often leading to adjournments or, in appropriate cases, the judge refusing to hear evidence from the party who has failed to comply with the order.

12 Fast Track (Part 28)

12.1 General

This track is for cases exceeding £5,000 and not exceeding £15,000 in value, where the trial will last no longer than a day. There are also limits on the amount of expert evidence, where allowed (see below). The objective is a trial date 20–30 weeks from issue. District judges and circuit judges have concurrent jurisdiction in fast track.

12.2 Allocation

Rule 26.6(5) and (6) provides:

(5) Subject to paragraph (6), the fast track is the normal track for any claim –

  (a) for which the small claims track is not the normal track; and

  (b) which has a financial value of not more than £15,000.

(6) The fast track is the normal track for the claims referred to in paragraph (5) only if the court considers that –

  (a) the trial is likely to last for no longer than one day; and

  (b) oral expert evidence at trial *(where allowed)* will be limited to –

    (i) one expert per party in relation to any expert field; and

    (ii) expert evidence in two expert fields.

The claim will *not* be allocated to this track if the court considers that the trial is likely to last longer than five hours (26PD9.1(3)(a)), taking account of the likely case management directions (see below), the court's powers to control evidence and limit cross-examination (see below) (26PD9.1(3)(b)) and whether any Part 20 claim is involved (see above, Chapter 8), as the time for this will be included in the estimate (26PD9.1(3)(e)).

The *mere possibility* that the trial may last longer than five hours or the fact that there is to be a split trial will not prevent allocation to this track (26PD9.1(3)(c) and (d)). However, if a case is *likely* to last more than one day, then the judge will consider allocating it to the multi-track, even though it is within the financial value for the fast track limit.

12.3 Directions (rule 28.2(1))

Once a defence has been filed and the matter allocated to the fast track, the district judge will scrutinise the papers to consider the following:

- whether further details of the claim or defence are necessary;
- whether the matter can be disposed of summarily (see above, Chapter 9);
- whether a preliminary hearing is necessary (at least three days' notice) (28PD3.10(1), 3.10(2));
- the question of venue.

The judge will take account of steps already taken by the parties and their compliance or non-compliance with any relevant pre-action protocol (28PD3.2; rule 28.2(1)).

In addition, the district judge will be responsible for:

- setting a timetable for the preparation and hearing of the case (see below, 12.4). The timetable can include strict limits on amounts of time for evidence, cross-examination and speeches;
- determining interlocutory applications;
- exercising discipline for failure to comply with procedural directions.

Note that unapproved local practice directions will not be permitted. This applies to all tracks.

12.3.1 'Typical' standard timetable (28PD3.12)

This will start from the date of service of the order for directions and may provide for:

- disclosure (see below, Chapter 16) – four weeks (rule 28.3);
- exchange of witness statements – 10 weeks (Rule 32.4, 28PD3.9(3));
- exchange of experts' reports – 14 weeks;
- dispatch of a listing questionnaire by the court (see below) – 20 weeks;
- return of questionnaire by parties (rule 28.5(1), 26PD9.2(1)) – 22 weeks;

- trial listed *30 weeks maximum* from the start date (rule 28.2(3) and (4)), with notification of the trial 'window' on allocation of not more than three weeks;
- trial date fixed not less than three weeks from notice to parties (rule 28.6(2)), unless the parties have agreed to accept shorter notice or, exceptionally, the court has ordered that shorter notice be given (28PD7.1(2)).

The parties must strive to co-operate with each other (28PD2.2) and may agree directions, provided that they comply with 28PD3.6 and 3.7 (28PD3.5), which broadly mirror the 'typical' timetable above.

Any party may apply either for an order compelling another to comply with a direction or for a sanction to be imposed, or for both (28PD5.1). The application must be made without delay but the other party should first be given a warning (28PD5.2).

12.4   The listing questionnaire (rule 28.5)

See below, Chapter 24, for a copy of this form.

Note rule 28.5:

(1) The court will send the parties a listing questionnaire for completion and return by the date specified in the notice of allocation unless it considers that the claim can be listed for trial without the need for a listing questionnaire ...

(3) The date specified for filing a listing questionnaire will not be more than 8 weeks before the trial date or the beginning of the trial period.

A fee of £200 is payable by the claimant on filing the listing questionnaire.

If neither party returns the listing questionnaire within 14 days of service, then, according to 28PD6.5(1), the court may make an order requiring return of the questionnaire within three days, in default of which the claim will be struck out. If only one party returns the listing questionnaire, then 28PD6.5(2) provides that the judge shall usually give listing directions or fix a listing hearing. If a listing hearing is directed, the court will fix a date which is as early as possible, giving the parties at least three days' notice (28PD6.3).

The court may give directions as to the issues on which evidence is to be given, the nature of the evidence it requires on those issues and the way in which it is to be placed before the court, and may thereby exclude evidence which would otherwise be admissible (rule 32.1).

A direction giving permission to use expert evidence will say whether it is to be by report or delivered orally, and will name the experts whose evidence is permitted (28PD7.2(4)). Permission may be made conditional on the experts discussing their differences and filing a report on the discussion.

12.5   Interlocutory hearings

These will, where possible, be avoided, but hearings will be needed in the following cases:

- where the court proposes to appoint an assessor (28PD3.11) (not so where the proposal is for a single joint expert) (see below, Chapter 18);
- where a party is dissatisfied with directions (28PD4.3);
- usually, on an application to enforce compliance (28PD5.1).

12.6   The importance of keeping the trial date

It is essential to note that the court will be very anxious to ensure that the trial date is maintained. See 28PD5.4 and, in particular:

> 5   Litigants and lawyers must be in no doubt that the court will regard the postponement of a trial as an order of last resort. The court may exercise its power to require a party as well as his legal representative to attend court at a hearing where such an order is to be sought.

An agreement between the parties to adjourn the trial date is not likely by itself to be enough to secure an adjournment.

12.7   Trial

The trial will normally take place at the court where the case is being managed, but it may be at another court if appropriate, having regard to the needs of the parties and the availability of court resources. It may be held away from court, if need be (28PD8.1, rule 2.7). Fast track cases are likely to be 'block listed' among a number of judges and courts; therefore, last minute changes of venue are possible.

All judges must properly have digested the papers *before trial* (28PD8.2). The trial bundle must be so put together as to assist such preparation (28PD7.2(2)(c) and see 39PD3).

The parties should attend all hearings with updated costs details, both of costs expended and those likely to be expended. The court may set a timetable for the trial and will confirm or vary the time estimate for the trial (rule 28.6(1)(b), 28PD7.2(2)(b)). No 'typical' timetable is suggested by the rules or practice. If the case has to go over from one day, it should, if possible, be heard the next day (28PD8.6). Evidence in chief will usually be by way of witness statement (rule 32.5(2)) and cross-examination can be curtailed (rule 32.1(3)).

12.8 Costs

See, also, below, Chapter 21.

The costs of fast track proceedings will usually be summarily assessed at the conclusion of the trial (28PD8.5). Thus, the parties will have been required to exchange costs details on the suggested form (See below, Chapter 24) at least 24 hours before the hearing.

There are fixed costs for the advocate on the trial, varying between £350 and £750, depending on the amount awarded in relation to the claimant and the amount claimed in relation to defendant, but this is not dependent on the length of the trial (rule 46.2):

Amount recovered (claimant) or claimed (defendant)	Fee
Up to £3000	£350
£3–10,000	£500
£10,000+	£750

A legal representative attending with counsel will be allowed £250 if his attendance was considered necessary (rule 46.3). However, should the case last longer than a day, no refresher is available – a clear incentive to finish within the time estimated.

12.9 Practical implications

• Fast track has proved the most problematical track for practitioners, not least because of the tight timetable and restrictions on expert evidence. This may explain why the number of cases settling in fast track is much higher than in any other track.

• Should practitioners find themselves in difficulty in complying with the timetable set by the court, they should not hesitate in applying to the court for an extension of time as soon as possible. The closer to the hearing date such an application is made, the less likely it is to be granted. In any event, where the court fixes directions, the parties have 14 days in which to object, failing which they may find that they are unable to do so.

- The court will resist doing anything which may result in the trial date or window being moved, unless the circumstances are truly exceptional, as to do otherwise would defeat the very object of a fast track hearing.

- The court will be required to consider not only the base costs at the end of the trial but also any dispute over the success fee where there is an additional liability (see below, Chapter 21). This may have the effect of extending the case beyond the one day maximum, which may have implications for adjournments and the advocates' fee (see above, 12.8).

13 Multi-Track

13.1 Venue

Civil trial centres are regionally situated and are supplemented by 'feeder', usually smaller, local county courts, who transfer multi-track cases to the centres. The centres are presided over by designated civil judges, who give guidance to the courts within their responsibility as to the application of the CPR and oversee their operation.

The court normally gives any directions appropriate upon allocation and then transfers the case to a civil trial centre; though it may either transfer to such a centre to deal with directions or, with the consent of the designated civil judge for the centre, retain the case for the time being for further management if it seems that there will be more than one case management conference and the parties' representatives are an inconvenient distance from the court (26PD10.2).

13.2 Steps on allocation

As for the definition of which cases are multi-track, see above, Chapters 1 and 10. Broadly speaking, it is for cases over £15,000 in value or those cases which do not fall into the other two tracks.

The procedural judge, on allocation, may do any or all of the following:

- issue written directions (rule 29.2(1)(a));
- set a timetable to fix, as appropriate:
  - o a case management conference (CMC);
  - o a pre-trial review (PTR) (rule 29.2(1)(b), 29PD4.5);
  - o a date for the filing of a completed listing questionnaire (rule 29.2(3)(b));
- set a trial date or a window for trial as soon as practicable (rule 29.2(2) and (3)(a)).

13.3   Directions

Directions, given at or without a hearing, will be tailored to the needs of the case and the steps already taken by the parties. The court will have regard to their compliance or non-compliance with any relevant pre-action protocol (29PD4.2). Its concern will be to ensure that the issues are identified and that the necessary evidence is prepared and disclosed (29PD4.3).

The court will expect the parties to co-operate in the giving of directions and may approve agreed directions which they submit (29PD4.6). See 29PD4.7, 4.8 for guidance on the agreed directions which may be approved.

The directions will deal with disclosure of documents (see below, Chapter 16), service of witness statements and expert evidence and may regulate amendments of statements of case (see above, Chapter 4) and the provision of further information. They should form a timetable for the steps to be taken through to the trial and make provision for the trial date or trial period (if not already fixed). In the absence of indications to the contrary, the court's general approach will be to direct (29PD4.10):

- filing and service of any further information need to clarify a party's case;
- standard disclosure;
- simultaneous exchange of witness statements;
- the instruction of a single joint expert on any appropriate issue; otherwise, simultaneous exchange of experts' reports (unless it is appropriate for reports on the amount of damages to be disclosed subsequently to those on liability); the court will not, however (save by agreement), require instruction of a single expert nor appoint an assessor without fixing a case management conference;
- discussion between experts and a statement thereon, if they are not agreed;
- a case management conference after the time for compliance; and
- the fixing of a trial period.

13.4   Case management conference (CMC) (29PD5)

The purpose of the CMC is to set the agenda for the case at the earliest possible stage, to ensure that the procedures followed and costs incurred are proportionate to the case. The court will fix a CMC if it appears that it cannot properly give directions on its own initiative and no agreed directions have been filed which it can approve. It will be listed as promptly as possible and at least three days' notice will be given.

The CMC is likely to involve:

- giving the parties directions on the future conduct of the case, including issues such as disclosure;
- establishing the likely timescale of the case, and may include setting dates for the milestone events, for example, a listing hearing, any further CMC, the return of the listing questionnaire or any pre-trial review;
- setting the trial date or trial window (if this has not already been done);
- agreeing a case summary (29PD5.7) (see below);
- exploring with the parties:
    - ○ the scope for settlement at this stage or the possibility of disposing of any particular issues;
    - ○ the extent to which experts will be needed, including the scope for using a single or joint expert and the need for oral evidence;
    - ○ the extent to which non-experts will be needed, and the need for oral evidence;
    - ○ whether there should be a split trial or trial of a preliminary issue (in which case, any directions would need to indicate to which aspect of the case they referred) (29PD5.3(7)); and
    - ○ whether the case should be tried by a High Court judge or a specialist judge (29PD5.9).

13.4.1 Attendance

If a party intends to apply for a particular direction which may be opposed, he should serve notice and, if the time allowed for the hearing may thus be insufficient, warn the court accordingly (29PD5.8).

If a party has legal representation, a representative familiar with the case and with sufficient authority to deal with any issues which may arise must attend (rule 29.3(2)). That person must be personally involved with the conduct of the case, and able to deal with fixing the timetable, identification of issues and matters of evidence (29PD5.2(2)). A wasted costs order will usually be made if the inadequacy of the person attending or his instructions leads to an adjournment (29PD5.3) (see below, Chapter 21).

Parties must ensure that all relevant documents (including witness statements and experts' reports) are available to the judge and that they all know what directions each of them seeks (29PD5.6). They should consider whether parties personally should attend and whether it would be useful to provide a *case summary* (prepared by the claimant and agreed with the other parties, if possible), setting out in 500 words a brief chronology, facts agreed and in dispute and evidence needed (29PD5.7).

13.5 Time for compliance

The time by which something is directed to be done may be varied by written agreement (rule 2.11), but this does not apply to (rule 29.5):

- the date fixed for a CMC or pre-trial review;
- the date for return of the listing questionnaire;
- the trial date or trial period; or
- any date, the variation of which would make it necessary to vary any of the above.

13.6 Preserving the trial date

As with fast track, it is important that, as far as possible, the trial date is maintained. Note 29PD7.4, in particular:

> 6 Litigants and lawyers must be in no doubt that the court will regard the postponement of a trial as an order of last resort. Where it appears inevitable the court may exercise its power to require a party as well as his legal representative to attend court at the hearing where such an order is to be sought.

13.7 Listing questionnaire

See below, Chapter 24, for a copy of the form.

Listing questionnaires completed by all parties will be required to be filed at some stage in the directions process, but in any case it is intended that they should be filed at least 10 weeks before the intended trial (rule 29.2(2)). The form of questionnaire is the same as for fast track (see above, Chapter 12).

The court will (unless it considers them unnecessary), in accordance with the procedural judge's directions, send a listing questionnaire to the parties (rule 29.6(1)) no later than two weeks before they are to be returned (29PD8.1(4)), which will be no later than eight weeks before the trial date or trial period (29PD8.1(3)). The parties are encouraged to exchange copies of their questionnaires before filing them, to avoid the court being given conflicting or incomplete information (29PD8.1(5)).

The listing questionnaire will help the court in deciding whether to fix a pre-trial review (rule 29.7) (see below). Where such a hearing has already been fixed, it will inform the parties as to whether that hearing is still required.

13.7.1 Decisions after return of questionnaire

On the basis of the information provided, the court will (rule 29.8, 29PD8.2):

* fix a pre-trial review (giving at least seven days' notice);
* cancel a previously fixed pre-trial review (rule 29.7);
* give listing directions;
* fix or confirm the trial date; and/or
* give any directions for the trial itself (including a trial timetable) which it considers appropriate.

13.7.2 Failure to respond

Where no party files a questionnaire, the court will normally order that, if none is filed within three days, the claim and any counterclaim be struck out (29PD8.3(1)). Otherwise, if a party fails to file his questionnaire, the court will fix a listing hearing on a date which is as early as possible (29PD8.3(2)), giving the parties at least three days' notice (29PD8.4). It will then normally fix or confirm the trial date and make other orders about steps to be taken to prepare the case for trial, whether or not the defaulting party attends (29PD8.3(2)).

13.8 Pre-trial review (rule 29.7)

This *may* be held by the eventual trial judge about eight to 10 weeks (variable) before the trial itself, in order to:

* resolve any discrepancies between the listing questionnaires;
* check that directions have been complied with;
* finalise the statement of issues to be tried. At the CMC, the court will already have endeavoured to narrow the issues to those relevant to be tried (see rule 1.4);

- confirm the hearing date;
- set the parameters for the trial, including:
  - ○ confirm which documents and case summaries need to be produced for the trial;
  - ○ where appropriate, fix the date by which any trial bundles should be lodged (usually seven days before the trial);
  - ○ its length and budget.

The court will give at least seven days' notice of its intention to hold a pre-trial review (rule 29.7). Sanctions for failure to comply with directions, orders or timetables will apply as with fast track (see 29PD7 and below, Chapter 12).

13.9   Listing directions

The court may give directions as follows:

- as to the issues on which evidence is to be given, the nature of the evidence it requires on those issues and the way in which it is to be placed before the court; it may thereby exclude evidence which would otherwise be admissible (rule 32.1);
- a direction giving permission to use expert evidence will say whether it is to be by report or orally and will name the experts whose evidence is permitted (29PD9.2(4));
- setting a timetable for the trial and confirm or vary trial date or week, the time estimate for the trial and the place of trial (rule 29.8(c)(i), 29PD9.1);
- for the preparation of a trial bundle (29PD9.2(2)(c)).

The parties should seek to agree the directions and file the proposed order (which will not bind the court) (29PD9.2(1)), making provision for the matters referred to above and any other matter needed to prepare for the trial (29PD9.2(2)).

13.10 The trial

Trial periods given in multi-track cases, instead of a fixture, are for a period of just one week only, rather than the possible three week period for fast track cases (rule 29.8(c)(ii)). As to conduct of the trial, see 29PD10.

13.11 Costs

There are no limits on costs on multi-track matters, once they have been allocated to that track, as there are in small claims and fast track cases. However, they are still subject to full scrutiny by the court in the light of the overriding objective and the principle of proportionality (see above, Chapter 1).

The costs will either be assessed summarily or by way of detailed assessment, and issues such as misconduct with regard to the proceedings can be raised (see below, Chapter 21).

13.12 Practical implications

- Multi-track is far less problematical than fast track, as the timetable is set by the court in co-operation with the parties and scaled to the size and complexity of the case. Similarly, directions will be tailored to the requirements of the case. Note, however, that the importance of maintaining the trial date is retained, as it is with fast track.

- Quite apart from giving case management directions, the judge is also empowered, and ought to take the opportunity, to explore the possibility of settlement between the parties. In the event of the judge expressing a view as part of settlement discussions, he/she ought to disqualify him/herself from dealing with the trial.

14 Interim Remedies (Part 25)

14.1 General

An application for an interim remedy may be made at any time; if urgent or 'otherwise desirable in the interests of justice', it may be made before a claim (rule 25.2(1)). Importantly, a draft of the order sought must be filed with the application and, if possible, a disk containing the draft should be available (in Word Perfect 5).

14.2 Scope of the remedy

Interim remedies are listed in rule 25(1) under three categories, viz, interim (formerly interlocutory) injunctions, declarations, and orders. Basically, the main orders relate to the detention, custody, preservation or inspection of property (rule 25.l(c)(i) and (ii)), for the sale or payment of income from property (rule 25.l(c)(v) and (vi)), for entry for the purpose of those orders (rule 25.1(d)), and for orders for delivery up of goods under s 4 of the Torts (Interference with Goods) Act 1977.

Interim orders may therefore be granted:

- for disclosure or inspection of property before a claim has been made;
- for interim payment which a defendant is held liable to pay, and for disputed funds to be paid into court;
- for payment into court on terms of release of property pending the outcome of proceedings relating to it;
- for accounts and inquiries.

14.3   Evidence

Unless otherwise ordered, any application for an interim injunction must be supported by evidence, and this must explain why notice has not been given if made without notice (rule 25.3). Provided that the application form itself contains the evidence which is verified by a statement of truth, that will suffice. Otherwise, it may be supported by evidence set out in a witness statement or in a statement of case verified by a statement of truth (25PD 3(1), (2) and (3)).

14.4   Interim remedies before the claim is issued

These can only be granted if the matter is urgent, or 'it is otherwise desirable to do so in the interests of justice' – a defendant must seek leave if his application is to be made before filing an acknowledgment of service or a defence (rule 25.2).

Before issue, applicants must undertake – subject to the court otherwise ordering – to issue a claim form immediately. This should, where possible, be served with the order (25PD4.4(2)). However, a claim form may not necessarily be directed where the application is only for pre-action disclosure (see below, Chapter 16).

14.5   Interim payments

Although more than one application for an interim payment can be made (rule 25.6(2)), no application can be made until the period for filing an acknowledgment of service has expired (rule 25.6(1)). Where the applicant is a child or patient, permission of the court must first be obtained (25PD IP1.2).

The application must (rule 25.6(3):

•   be served at least 14 days before the hearing;

•   be supported by evidence.

25PD IP2.1 sets out what the evidence must deal with:

1   the sum of money sought by way of an interim payment,

2   the items or matters in respect of which the interim payment is sought,

3   the sum of money for which final judgment is likely to be given,

4   the reasons for believing that the conditions set out in rule 25.7 are satisfied,

5   any other relevant matters,

6   in claims for personal injuries, details of special damages and past and future loss, and

7   in a claim under the Fatal Accidents Act 1976, details of the person(s) on whose behalf the claim is made and the nature of the claim.

Any relevant documents should be exhibited, including, in a personal injuries case, the medical report (25PD IP 2.2). Any response by way of written evidence must be filed and served at least seven days before the hearing (rule 25.6(4)).

The court will only make an interim payment order if:

- liability is admitted either in whole or in part (rule 25.7(1)(a)); or
- judgment has already been obtained (rule 25.7(1)(b)); or
- the court is satisfied that, if the matter went to trial, the claimant would obtain a substantial judgment (rule 25.7(1)(c)) (see below for the position where there is more than one defendant); or
- it is a claim for possession and the defendant would be liable to pay for use and occupation (rule 25.7(1)(d)).

Where the claim is for personal injuries, an interim payment can only be ordered if:

- the defendant is insured; or
- the Motor Insurers Bureau are dealing with the claim; or
- the defendant is a public body (rule 25.7(2)).

Where the claim is for possession, an interim payment can only be ordered if the defendant would be liable to pay for use and occupation (rule 25.7(1)(d)).

Where there is more than one defendant in a personal injury case, the court must also be satisfied that the claimant would obtain judgment against at least one of them (rule 25.7(3)). Although the court can take into account contributory negligence and any set-off or counterclaim (rule 25.7(5)), nevertheless the amount of the interim payment should not be more than 'a reasonable proportion of the likely amount of the final judgment' (rule 25.7(4)).

The amount of the interim payments is taken into account on the final judgment and any necessary adjustments made (25PD IP5). Once an interim payment has been ordered, the court can make orders for repayment, where necessary (rule 25.8).

14.6 Freezing injunction (formerly Mareva injunction)

This is an order to restrain a party from removing from the jurisdiction assets located there, or from dealing with assets wherever located. The High Court alone has jurisdiction, except if there is an authorised judge. The same applies to search orders (see below) (25PD1.1) However, there is jurisdiction for any master or district judge to make an order in the High Court if it is:

- by consent;
- in connection with charging orders and appointments of receivers;
- in aid of execution (25PD1.3).

Therefore, if a freezing or search order is required in a county court case, the case should be transferred to the High Court to obtain the order. The case can then, if appropriate, be transferred back to the county court.

14.7 Search order (formerly Anton Piller order)

Note that these are also the preserve of the High Court.

The county court has been empowered, most recently by s 67 of the Civil Procedure Act 1997, to make an order to secure the preservation of evidence or of property. Such an order can only be exercised by 'a supervising solicitor' experienced in their operation (see 25PD7).

14.8 Cesser of interim injunctions

If the court has granted an interim injunction and the action is subsequently stayed, the injunction shall cease to have effect unless the court orders otherwise (rule 25.10). If the claim is struck out, the interim injunction comes to an end 14 days thereafter (rule 25.11).

14.9 Security for costs

An application for costs may be made by a defendant under rule 25.12. It must be supported by written evidence (rule 25.12(2)). The grounds for the application are set out in rule 25.13(2):

The conditions are –

(a) the claimant is an individual –

     (i)   who is ordinarily resident out of the jurisdiction; and

     (ii) is not a person against whom a claim can be enforced under the Brussels Conventions or the Lugano Convention, as defined by s 1(1) of the Civil Jurisdiction and Judgments Act 1982;

(b) the claimant is a company or other incorporated body –

     (i)   which is ordinarily resident out of the jurisdiction; and

     (ii) is not a body against whom a claim can be enforced under the Brussels Conventions or the Lugano Convention;

(c) the claimant is a company or other body (whether incorporated inside or outside Great Britain) and there is reason to believe that it will be unable to pay the defendant's costs if ordered to do so;

(d) the claimant has changed his address since the claim was commenced with a view to evading the consequences of the litigation;

(e) the claimant failed to give his address in the claim form, or gave an incorrect address in that form;

(f) the claimant is acting as a nominal claimant, other than as a representative claimant under Part 19, and there is reason to believe that he will be unable to pay the defendant's costs if ordered to do so;

(g) the claimant has taken steps in relation to his assets that would make it difficult to enforce an order for costs against him.

The defendant may seek an order for security for costs against any other person, if the court considers it appropriate, if that person assigned their right to claim to the claimant so as to avoid a costs order being made against them (for example, a company assigning a right to a director who can apply for funding assistance) or has agreed to contribute to the claimant's costs in return for a share in anything recovered (rule 25.14).

The court may order security for costs of an appeal (rule 25.15).

14.10 Practical implications

- Any application for interim relief should be made as soon as it is considered necessary, as any delay may affect the efficacy of the application.

- The court will usually assess costs (but not any additional liability – see below, Chapter 21) on a summary basis at the end of the application, so practitioners should ensure that they have prepared and served the necessary schedules of costs (see below, Chapter 21). The advantage of such summary assessment is that it enables the receiving party to collect costs 'as they go', as the costs will be payable within 14 days of the order, unless the court orders otherwise.

15 Applications

15.1 General

Applications made during a claim, or before a claim is commenced, are made in accordance with Part 23. Part 32 deals with evidence at interlocutory hearings.

Certain specific applications are dealt with in the following parts:

- to add or substitute a party – Part 19 (see below);
- to make other amendments – Part 17 (see above, Chapter 4);
- for a consent order – Part 40;
- for summary judgment – Part 24 (see above, Chapter 9);
- for further information – Part 18 (see below);
- to change solicitor – Part 42;
- for interim remedies – Part 25 (see above, Chapter 14).

15.2 Procedure

Applications should be made:

- as soon as the need becomes apparent (23PD2.7);
- wherever possible so that they can be considered at any other hearing, whether arranged or anticipated – for example, case management conferences, allocation and listing hearings and pre-trial reviews fixed by the court (rule 1.4(2)(1) – the overriding objective) (23PD2.8);
- with the knowledge that the court may wish to review the conduct of the case as a whole and give any necessary case management directions (23PD2.9).

The application is made by filing an application notice, unless a rule or practice direction provides otherwise, or the court dispenses with one (rule 23.3). Where a date for a hearing has been fixed and a party wishes to make an application at that hearing but does not have sufficient time to serve an application notice, he should inform the other party and the court as soon as he can (in writing, if possible) of the nature of the application and the reason for it. He should then make the application orally at the hearing (23PD2.10).

An application notice must state:
* if it is intended to be made to a circuit judge or district judge;
* what order the applicant seeks;
* brief reasons for the application;
* the title of the claim;
* the reference number of the claim;
* the full name of the applicant;
* where the applicant is not already a party, his address for service;
* a request for a hearing, or that the application be dealt with without a hearing (rule 23.6 and 23PD1 and 2).

Generally, a copy of the application notice must be served as soon as practicable after it is filed and, in any event, at least three clear days before the hearing, unless another time limit is prescribed by a rule or practice direction (23PD4). An application may be made without serving an application notice (formerly known as *ex parte*) only:
* where there is exceptional urgency;
* where the overriding objective is best furthered by doing so;
* by consent of all parties;
* with the permission of the court;
* where para 2.10 applies; that is, where a date for a hearing has been fixed and a party wishes to make an application at that hearing but he does not have sufficient time to serve an application notice, he should inform the other party and the court (if possible in writing) as soon as he can of the nature of the application and the reason for it. He should then make the application orally at the hearing; or
* where a court order, rule or Practice Direction permits (23PD3).

Evidence at interlocutory hearings is given in writing by witness statement, statement of case and/or application notice (if the latter is verified by a statement of truth – rule 32.6(2)), unless the court orders otherwise (rule 32.6). Affidavit evidence may be used but, unless the court has ordered it or a rule requires it, any additional cost may not be recovered from another party (rule 32.15). Any evidence on which the applicant seeks to rely must be filed and served with the application notice, unless it has already been filed and served (23PD9.3).

23PD10 sets out the procedure for dealing with consent orders.

15.3 Further information (rule 18)

This replaces the previous rules on requests for further and better particulars and interrogatories. Note rule 18.1:

(1) The court may at any time order a party to –

(a) clarify any matter which is in dispute in the proceedings; or

(b) give additional information in relation to any such matter, whether or not the matter is contained or referred to in a statement of case.

The court may exercise this power either on its own initiative or on application by a party. Before seeking such an order, there should have first been a request in writing to the other side, who should be given a reasonable amount of time in which to respond (18PD1 and 2). Although the application must usually be made on notice, in accordance with Part 23 (18PD5.1), where the respondent does not reply to the request (minimum period 14 days), the application may be made without notice (18PD5.5).

15.4 Adding or substituting a party (rule 19)

The new rules are similar to the old ones; application is required and can be by any party, or intended party, with a hearing, or by consent. Note rule 19.1:

(2) The court may order a person to be added as a new party if –

(a) it is desirable to add the new party so that the court can resolve all the matters in dispute in the proceedings; or

(b) there is an issue involving the new party and an existing party which is connected to the matters in dispute in the proceedings, and it is desirable to add the new party so that the court can resolve that issue.

(3) The court may order any person to cease to be a party if it is not desirable for that person to be a party to the proceedings.

(4) The court may order a new party to be substituted for an existing one if –

  (a) the existing party's interest or liability has passed to the new party; and

  (b) it is desirable to substitute the new party so that the court can resolve the matters in dispute in the proceedings.

The court has a very wide discretion as to whether to make the order. As with amendments generally (see Part 17 and above, Chapter 4), it is likely that the application will be granted if it does not cause injustice to other parties which cannot otherwise be compensated by costs (*Beoco Ltd v Alfa Laval Co Ltd* [1994] All ER 464, CA) and the principles of the overriding objective are upheld.

The Practice Direction makes it clear that a party applying for an amendment will usually be responsible for the costs of and arising from the amendment.

15.5   Adding and substituting parties

15.5.1   New claimant

The applicant must file (rule 19.3 and see the Practice Direction thereto):
- the application;
- proposed amended claim form;
- proposed amended Particulars of Claim;
- written consent of new claimant.

15.5.2   New defendants

These are to be served with (19PD3.2(3)):
- a copy of the order;
- the amended claim form and amended Particulars of Claim; and
- the 'response pack' (see above, Chapter 7).

15.5.3 Special provisions (rule 19.4)

Special provisions apply regarding adding or substituting after the end of a period of limitation under the Limitation Act 1980. An order can only be obtained if the limitation period was current when the proceedings were 'started' and the substitution or addition 'is necessary' on the court being satisfied that the party previously named was by mistake for the new correct party, and, unless the new party is added or substituted, the claim cannot properly be carried on by, or against, the original party; or where the original party has died or had a Bankruptcy Order made against him.

For personal injury claims and fatal accidents, see ss 11 and 12 of the Limitation Act 1980. For circumstances in which a new cause of action may be introduced, see s 35 of the same Act.

15.6 Practical implications

* With case management being taken over by the court, the need for interim procedural applications has diminished somewhat.

* The courts are now much more prepared to consider applications to enforce existing directions on paper only, avoiding the need for a hearing. This includes applications under rule 42(3) by solicitors to come off the record, unless the matter is particularly complex. The courts are also encouraging parties to deal with applications by way of telephone conferences, and many judges' chambers have been provided suitable equipment to enable them to conduct such conferences. An option to select a telephone conference is included on the application form.

* As with interim remedies (see above, Chapter 14), practitioners are reminded of the need to prepare and serve schedules of costs for summary assessment, as costs are likely to be so assessed at the end of the application.

16 Disclosure

16.1   General

'Disclosure' replaces the old 'discovery'. The new rules are in Part 31 of the CPR 1998, which applies to all claims except those on the small claims track, and provide for 'standard disclosure'. Disclosure is confined to those documents which are, or have been, in a party's control, viz, actually with him, or of which he has a right to possession or inspect or take copies (rule 31.8). Disclosure means 'stating that the document exists or has existed' and with it there is an automatic right to inspection of such a document unless the party no longer controls the documents or claims the right to withhold inspection (rule 31.2).

'Document' means anything in which information of any description is recorded, and 'copy' means 'anything onto which information recorded in the document has been copied by whatever means and whether directly or indirectly' (rule 31.4).

16.2   Standard disclosure

There is now 'standard disclosure' by virtue of rule 31.6, and this requires a party to disclose:

- all documents on which he relies;
- all documents of which he is aware which could adversely affect his own case or adversely affect or support another party's case;
- and whatever may be required by any Practice Direction.

Rule 31.5(1) provides that, during proceedings, 'an order to give disclosure is an order to give standard disclosure unless the court orders otherwise'.

Rule 31.3(2) provides:

Where a party considers that it would be disproportionate to the issues in the case to permit inspection of documents within a category or class of document disclosed under rule 31.6(b):

(a) he is not required to permit inspection of documents within that category or class; but

(b) he must state in his disclosure statement that inspection of those documents will not be permitted on the grounds that to do so would be disproportionate.

16.3   Procedure for standard disclosure

A list identifying the documents in a convenient order and as concisely as possible – indicating those documents which are no longer in the party's control and what has happened to such documents – must be served on every other party. The list is to be in Form N265.

Notwithstanding the stated requirement to serve a list, parties may always agree, in writing, to disclose documents without making a list or a disclosure statement, for example, by referring to them in a letter, and they may also similarly agree to dispense with a 'disclosure statement' (rule 31.10(8)) (see below). The party making disclosure should list the documents in date order, number them consecutively and give each a concise description (for example, 'letter claimant to defendant'). Where there is a large number of documents all falling into a particular category, the disclosing party may list those documents as a category rather than individually, for example:

50 bank statements relating to account number .... at X Bank, ... 20... to .... 20...

Or:

35 letters passing between X and Y between .... 20... and .... 20...

Added to the list of documents is a 'disclosure statement'. This is required by rule 31.10(5). Rule 31.10(6) provides that a disclosure statement is a document which:

(a) sets out the extent of the search that has been made to locate documents which the party is required to disclose;

(b) certifies that the party understands the duty to disclose;

(c) certifies that the party has carried out that duty to the best of his knowledge.

Preferably, this document should be signed by someone with actual knowledge of the contents. In the case of businesses, the disclosure statement must identify the person making the statement and explain why he is considered to be the appropriate person (rule 31.10(7)).

By sub-rule (8), the parties can agree in writing to waive the making of a formal list and the requirement to provide the disclosure statement. The duty of disclosure continues during the whole of the proceedings, so that any documents that come to a party's notice must immediately be disclosed (rule 31.11), with the duty to disclose being immediate. However, discovery may be in 'stages', at the direction of the court or by agreement of the parties (rule 31.13).

16.4   The duty to search

Rule 31.7 provides that, when giving standard disclosure, a party is required to 'make a reasonable search for documents falling within rule 31.6(b) or (c)'. What amounts to reasonableness is defined in sub-rule (2). This involves consideration of:

- the number of documents involved;
- the nature and complexity of the proceedings;
- the ease and expense of retrieval of a particular document;
- the significance of any document likely to be located,

and, it is suggested, the overriding objective under Part 1.

Disproportionality is relevant, except that, this time, it is called 'unreasonableness' (this is wider than disproportionality but includes it). Rule 31.7(3) provides:

> Where a party has not searched for a category or class of document on the grounds that to do so would be unreasonable, he must state this in his disclosure statement and identify the category or class of document.

The search can be limited by date, location or category but any limitation must be stated in the 'disclosure statement' (see above). This will enable the other side to be aware of the limits of the search and challenge it, if necessary.

16.5   Specific disclosure

The court may always make an order for specific disclosure, that is, to disclose documents or classes of documents specified in the order, or to carry out a search to such extent as may be stated in the order, and to disclose any documents located as a result of that search (rule 31.12). Whenever a party wishes to apply for an order for specific disclosure, such application must be supported 'by evidence' and grounds must be given (31PD5.1) (see above, Chapter 15).

31PD5.1 gives the only ground for an application for specific disclosure as inadequate disclosure by the other party. 'Fishing expeditions' are unlikely to succeed, especially as the application has to be supported by evidence.

16.6   Disclosure of documents referred to in other documents

Note Rule 31.14:

A party may inspect a document mentioned in –

(a) a Statement of Case;

(b) a Witness Statement;

(c) a Witness Summary;

(d) an Affidavit; or

(e) subject to rule 35.10(4), an Expert's Report.

If the documents are not in the possession of the respondent, the applicant might wish to apply for non-party disclosure (rule 31.17) or for a deposition or witness summons (rule 34.2(4)(b)).

16.7   Inspection

Except where the document is no longer in the control of the party who disclosed it, or that party has a right, or a duty, to withhold inspection of it, a party to whom a document has been disclosed has the right to inspect that document (rule 31.3). They must have first given the party who disclosed the document written notice of the wish to inspect, when inspection must be given within seven days. If they undertake to pay reasonable copying charges, a party may request a copy, which, again, must be supplied within seven days.

Note Rule 31.15:

The right to inspect includes documents mentioned in the Statement of Case, or in Witness Statements or Summaries, in Affidavits or in Experts' Reports.

16.8 Pre-proceedings disclosure

On the application of a person who is likely to be a party in proceedings in which a claim is likely to be made, the court may order another person who is likely to be a party and to have or have had in his control documents relevant to an issue arising out of the claim, to disclose whether he has such documents in his control and, if so, to produce them to the applicant's legal, medical or other professional advisers (but not to the applicant personally) (s 33 of the Supreme Court Act (SCA) 1981; s 52 of the County Courts Act (CCA) 1984). The Civil Procedure (Modification of Enactments) Order 1998 (SI 1998/2940) provides that the application can now be made in anticipation of any type of proceedings and is no longer limited to personal injury claims.

16.8.1 Procedure (rule 25.4)

- The application is made by application notice, not by issuing a claim (see above, Chapter 15).
- The application must be supported by evidence.
- The documents sought must be such as would fall to be disclosed by standard disclosure, were proceedings commenced between the applicant and respondent.
- The disclosure must be desirable in order to dispose fairly of the anticipated proceedings, to assist the dispute being resolved without proceedings or to save costs.
- The order will specify the documents or classes of documents to be disclosed and require the respondent to say which (if any) of the specified documents are no longer in his control and in respect of which he claims a right or duty to withhold inspection. It may require him to say what has happened to any which are no longer in his control, and may specify the time and place for disclosure and inspection.
- If the court makes the order, it may give directions requiring a claim to be commenced – but need not do so.

16.9 Disclosure against non-parties (rule 31.17)

In any proceedings, the court may, on application, order a person who is not a party but is likely to have in his control documents relevant to an issue arising out of the claim to disclose whether he has such documents in his control and, if so, to produce them to the applicant's legal, medical or other professional advisers (but not to the applicant personally) (s 34 of the SCA 1981; s 53 of the CCA 1984).

16.9.1 Procedure

- The application must be supported by evidence (rule 31.17(2)) (see above, Chapter 15).

- The documents sought must be likely to support the case of the applicant or adversely affect that of another party (rule 31.17(3)(a)).

- The disclosure must be necessary in order to dispose fairly of the claim or to save costs (rule 31.17(3)(b)).

- The order will specify the documents or classes of documents to be disclosed and require the respondent to say which (if any) of the specified documents are no longer in his control and in respect of which he claims a right or duty to withhold inspection (rule 31.17(4)).

- The order may also require the respondent to say what has happened to any which are no longer in his control and may specify the time and place for disclosure and inspection (rule 31.17(5)).

16.10 Non-disclosure

Rule 31.21 states that 'A party may not rely on any document which he fails to disclose or in respect of which he fails to permit inspection unless the Court permits'. This is intended to encourage early and proper disclosure.

16.11 Subsequent use of disclosed documents

Rule 31.22 makes it clear that a party to whom a document has been disclosed may use the document only for the purpose of proceedings in which it is disclosed, unless the document has been read to or by the court or been referred to during a hearing in public. Even then, the court may make an order restricting or prohibiting the use of the document.

16.12 Practical implications

Disclosure has proved to be one of the least problematical aspects of the new procedures. There have only been two major cases reported on disclosure, one of which dealt with the old issue of inadvertent disclosure of privileged documents and the other declaring *ultra vires* the provision requiring parties to make privileged documents available if challenged as part of the costs process, which provision was subsequently amended.

Matters have proceeded very much as before, save that the courts have been anxious to keep documents down to those absolutely necessary and to be relied upon in court.

17 Evidence

17.1   Court's control of evidence

The courts now have expanded power to control evidence. Rule 32.1 states:

(1) The court may control the evidence by giving directions as to –

    (a) the issues on which it requires evidence;

    (b) the nature of the evidence which it requires to decide those issues; and

    (c) the way in which the evidence is to be placed before the court.

(2) The court may use its power under this rule to exclude evidence that would otherwise be admissible.

(3) The court may limit cross-examination.

Directions as to the control of evidence may be given at any stage, but, more usually, are given on allocation or at a pre-trial review.

17.2   Hearsay evidence

This is always admissible but its value may be questioned.

The Rules (rule 33.1) define hearsay as 'a statement made otherwise than by a person while giving oral evidence in the proceedings, which is tendered as evidence of the matters stated'; basically, then, not the direct evidence of a witness himself, but what someone else has been heard to say. If a statement is made – other than by a witness in the course of giving his evidence – evidence of it can be given to prove that the statement was made, and that is not hearsay; but it cannot be offered as proof of its contents – that would be hearsay.

Section 1 of the Civil Evidence Act 1995 provides that, in civil proceedings, evidence shall not be excluded on the grounds that it is hearsay. Section 2(l)(a) states that a party intending to adduce hearsay evidence 'shall' give notice of that fact; such has been the requirement since the Civil Evidence Act 1968 came into force.

Section 2(4) of the 1995 Act goes on to say that *failure* to give notice may be taken into account in considering the weight to be given to the evidence, and is also relevant in considering award of costs, but does not affect the admissibility of the evidence. Thus, there is no power to actually exclude evidence which is hearsay, assuming that it is relevant, under any circumstances.

17.2.1 The 'hearsay notice'

There are two circumstances under which reliance on hearsay evidence needs to be considered: when notice is required and when it is not.

Notice required (rule 33.2)

(1) Where a party intends to rely on hearsay evidence at trial and either –

  (a) that evidence is to be given by a witness giving oral evidence; or

  (b) that evidence is contained in a witness statement of a person who is not being called to give oral evidence;

  that party complies with s 2(1)(a) of the Civil Evidence Act 1995 by serving a witness statement on the other parties in accordance with the court's order.

(2) Where paragraph (1)(b) applies, the party intending to rely on the hearsay evidence must, when he serves the witness statement, inform the other   parties that the witness is not being called to give oral evidence.

(3) In all other cases where a party intends to rely on hearsay evidence at trial, that party complies with s 2(1)(a) of the Civil Evidence Act 1995 by serving a notice on the other parties which –

  (a) identifies the hearsay evidence; and

  (b) states that the party serving the notice proposes to rely on the hearsay evidence at trial.

(4) The party proposing to rely on the hearsay evidence must –

  (a) serve the notice no later than the latest date for serving witness statements; and

(b) if the hearsay evidence is to be in a document, supply a copy to any party who requests him to do so.

Notice not required (rule 33.3)

Section 2(1) of the Civil Evidence Act 1995 (duty to give notice of intention to rely on hearsay evidence) does not apply –

(a) to evidence at hearings other than trials;

(b) to a statement which a party to a probate action wishes to put in evidence and which is alleged to have been made by the person whose estate is the subject of the proceedings; or

(c) where the requirement is excluded by a practice direction.

An opposing party's application to cross-examine in respect of hearsay may be made within 14 days after a notice to rely on hearsay has been given; the power of the court extends to allowing the opposing party to call the maker of a hearsay statement (rule 33.4(1) and (2)).

Where the party relying on the hearsay statement does not himself propose to call the maker of it, the opposing party can give notice of his intention to call his evidence to attack the maker's credibility (rule 33.5(1)).

17.3 Different types of evidence

17.3.1 Admissions (rule 14)

A fact may be admitted on the pleadings; an opponent may make use of the admittance by himself averring it with a different interpretation. Formal admissions may also be made in response to a notice to admit, or in answer to a request for further information (Part 18 – see above, Chapter 15). Admissions may be made at any stage, as well as at the trial itself. Formal admissions made in civil proceedings are binding only for the purpose of those proceedings.

17.3.2 Non-expert evidence

This is set out in Part 32. Rule 32.1(1) states that it is for the court to give directions as to the issues on which evidence is required as to the nature of the evidence required on those issues and the way in which the evidence is to be placed before the court. Rule 32.1(2) states that 'the Court may use its power as under this rule to exclude evidence that would otherwise be admissible'. The general principle is that evidence of witnesses is to be proved:

- at trial, by oral evidence in public;
- at any other hearing, by written evidence.

Evidence may be given by video link or by 'any other means' (rule 32.3) (see below).

17.3.3 Witness statements

The court is given the power to order a party to serve on any other party a witness statement of the oral evidence which the party serving the statement intends to rely on in relation to any issues of fact to be decided at trial.

A witness statement is a 'written statement which contains the evidence and only that evidence which a person will be allowed to give orally at trial' (rule 32.4). It must also be verified by a *statement of truth* – 'A certificate by its maker that he believes the statement of fact in it are true' (32PD20 and Part 22; see above, Chapter 4). For the format of witness statements, see 32PD17–24. Failure to comply with the formalities may result in a refusal of the court to admit the document or to allow the costs of preparation (32PD25).

Under rule 32.4(2) and (3), the court can give directions as to the order in which witness statements are to be served and whether or not witness statements are to be filed. The normal situation will be for a witness whose statement has been served to give evidence orally in court (rule 32.5(1)). The written witness statement is to stand as the evidence in chief, unless the court orders otherwise (rule 32.5(2)).

In giving oral evidence at trial, the witness may, with the permission of the court (and if the court thinks that there is good reason (rule 32.5(4)):

- amplify the witness statement;
- give evidence in relation to new matters which have arisen since the witness statement was served on the other parties (rule 32.5(3)).

If a party who has served a witness statement does not call the witness or put in the witness statement as hearsay (see above), the other party may put in the witness statement as hearsay evidence (rule 32.5(5)).

17.3.4 Witness summaries as an alternative

Witness summaries may be served with the court's leave on application without notice where it is not possible to obtain a witness statement (rule 32.9(1)). The intention is to be able to refer to brief notes obtained and prepared which do not go quite so far as the full statement, but rule 32.9(2)(b) provides that the document may also be a summary of 'matters about which the party serving the witness summary will question the witness'. This will therefore apply in the hostile witness situation. The rules as to service, amplification and form are the same as for witness statements (rule 32.9(4)(5)).

Rule 32.10 provides that, if a witness statement for use at trial (or a witness summary) is not served in respect of an intended witness within the time specified by the court, then the witness may not be called to give oral evidence *unless the court permits*.

17.4 Attendance of witnesses

A witness summons to secure attendance may be issued at any time, except that, where a party wishes to have a summons issued less than seven days before the date of the trial, he must obtain permission from the court, and in certain other exceptional cases (rule 34.3(1), (2)). A witness summons is to be issued in the court where the case is proceedings, or where the hearing will be held (rule 34.3(3)).

Witness summonses are to be served by the court, unless the party on whose behalf it is issued indicates in writing, when he asks the court to issue, that he wishes to serve it himself (rule 34.6(1)). Where the court is to serve the witness summons, the party on whose behalf it is issued must deposit in the court office the money to be paid or offered to the witness under rule 34.7 (see below) (rule 34.6(2)).

At the time of service, the witness must be offered or paid a sum reasonably sufficient to cover his expenses in travelling to and from the court, and such sum by way of compensation for loss of time as may be specified in the relevant Practice Direction (rule 34.7) (see 34PD3, Witness Attendance). It is important to note that a witness summons may be set aside by the court which issues it, and the person served with a witness summons may apply.

17.5   Affidavits

Evidence is to be given by affidavit if it is required by the court, practice direction or any other enactment, or as an alternative to witness statements or in addition to it, if the court requires it (rule 32.15(1)). An affidavit may be used in circumstances where a statement would have sufficed, but the party putting it forward may not recover any additional costs of preparing it, unless the court otherwise orders (rule 32.15(2)). For the format of affidavits, see 32PD2–16. Failure to comply with the formalities may have the same result as with witness statements (see above).

17.6   Notices to admit facts and/or documents

These are available, as previously, under rule 32.18 and 19. A notice to admit facts must be served no later than 21 days before trial (rule 32.18(2)), while a notice to prove a document must be served by the latest date for serving witness statements or within seven days of disclosure of the document, whichever is later (rule 32.19(2)).

17.7   Plans, photographs and models

For trial, to ensure that plans, etc, can be received in evidence, notice of intention to make use of the plans, models, etc, must be given 14 days before date for serving witness statements, if they are part of witness statements, affidavits or expert's reports In other cases, the time period is 21 days before the hearing (rule 33.6).

17.8   Video

The use of video equipment is expressly referred to at rule 32.3: 'The court may allow a witness to give evidence through a video link or by other means.' It is also mentioned in para 7 of the Practice Direction to Part 23:

Video Conferencing

7   Where the parties to a matter wish to use video conferencing facilities, and those facilities are available in the relevant court, they should apply to the Master or District Judge for directions.

Video links are currently being considered by the Court Service as part of their overall IT strategy. See, also, *QB Masters Practice Direction No 50 – Applications to QB Masters by Video Conference.*

17.9 Practical implications

- Even before the new Rules were formulated, the use of witness statements had found favour with the courts. They cut down drastically on the need for evidence in chief and enabled mutual disclosure of each party's case, which married well with the joint co-operation that is a feature of the CPR.

- Indeed, the importance of witness statements has increased almost to the same degree as 'pleadings' have decreased in terms of forming the substance of each party's case, a matter commented on by Lord Woolf himself, who described pleadings as being of 'historical value only' in the light of the increased use of witness statements.

- The verification of statements of case by statements of truth has also turned them into admissible evidence, which avoids the need for extraneous evidence in some instances, for example, summary judgment, unless necessary.

- Witness statements have now taken over from affidavits as the main source of admissible written evidence. Care should be taken over their preparation to ensure that they properly reflect the evidence of the witness who is providing the evidence and, as far as possible, to ensure that they are in the witness's own words. Thus, lay witnesses ought not to be expected to propound arguments as to the law in their evidence of the facts.

- As witness statements have become of considerable importance, it is not surprising that the courts are prepared to penalise those who fail to comply with orders for their production, even to the extent of refusing to hear evidence which has not previously been provided in a disclosed statement.

18 Experts and Assessors

18.1 General

The adversarial nature of expert evidence in litigation is abolished, and now the expert's primary duty is to help the court, and to override any obligation to those who may have instructed or paid him. Rule 35.1 demands that:

> Expert evidence shall be restricted to that which is reasonably required to resolve the proceedings.

Most importantly, the duty of the expert to the court is the overriding duty. Rule 35.3 states:

(1) It is the duty of an expert to help the Court on the matters within his expertise.

(2) This duty overrides any obligation to the person from whom he has received instructions or by whom he is paid.

The court will not direct an expert to attend in fast track cases, 'unless it is necessary to do so in the interests of justice'. In 'small claims', neither written nor oral expert evidence may be adduced without the permission of the court. Experts' fees, if any, in small claims are limited to the amount specified in 27PD7.3, that is, £200.

18.2 Access to the court

The expert is now given direct access to the court to assist him carrying out his functions as an expert to the court. An expert has the right to seek directions from the court without giving notice to either party (rule 35.14). However, the court may direct that a copy of the request and of the directions given be served on the parties when the directions are given.

18.3   Single expert

The court has an overriding power to decide that evidence before it should be given by a *single joint expert,* rather than the party's individual experts (rule 35.7). Where two or more parties want to submit expert evidence on a particular issue, the court may direct that the evidence on that issue be given by one expert only. Where the parties cannot agree who should be the expert, the court will decide from a list prepared or identified by the parties, or may choose an expert in some other manner (rule 35.7(3)). Instructions for the single joint expert appointed in this manner comes from both parties. The party must exchange their respective instructions (rule 35.8).

Liability to pay the fees of the expert will be joint and several, unless the court has ordered otherwise. The court has a right to give directions about the arrangements of the payment of the experts fees and may limit the amount that can be paid by way of fees and expenses.

The 'written questions' provision (see below) is available, enabling the parties to raise and clarify points with the expert. This is particularly useful in fast track cases, where the single joint expert is likely to be the rule rather than the exception.

18.4   Form and content of reports

See the Practice Direction to Part 35, 1.1–1.6 for details. The contents reflect the new regime and remind the expert of both his duty to the court and the need to be neutral. The report must (35PD1.2):

(2) give details of any literature or other material which the expert has relied on in making the report,

(3) say who carried out any test or experiment which the has used for the report and whether or not the test or experiment has been carried out under the expert's supervision,

(4) give the qualifications of the person who carried out any such test or experiment, and

(5) where there is a range of opinion on the matters dealt with in the report –

(i) summarise the range of opinion, and

(ii) give reasons for his own opinion,

(6) contain a summary of the conclusions reached,

(7) contain a statement that the expert understands his duty to the court and has complied with that duty (Rule 35.10(2)), and

(8) contain a statement setting out the substance of all material instructions (whether written or oral). The statement should summarise the facts and instructions given to the expert which are material to the opinions expressed in the report or upon which those opinions are based (Rule 35.10(3)).

The Report should conclude: 'I believe that the facts I have stated in this report are true and that the opinions I have expressed are correct,' and there must be a final statement in any report that the expert understands his duty to the court and has complied with that duty.

The report must also state the substance of all material instructions, including oral instructions upon which the report was written. Instructions are therefore no longer privileged against disclosure (rule 35.11). However, the rules do provide that the court will not order disclosure of any specific document referred to or permit examination of the expert in relation to the instructions, unless the court is satisfied that there are reasonable grounds to consider that the statement of instructions contained in the report may be incomplete. A party may use another disclosed report on which the instructing party does not rely to support their case if so desired.

18.5 Questions to experts

Note Rule 35.6:

The Court may permit, or the parties may agree, to put pertinent questions, otherwise they are to be asked only to clarify.

See, also, 35PD4.1 and 4.2:

4.1 Questions asked for the purpose of CLARIFYING the expert's report (see Rule 35.6) should be put, in writing, to the expert not later than 28 days after receipt of the expert's report (see paras 1.2 to 1.5 above as to verification).

4.2 Where a party sends a written question or questions direct to an expert and the other party is represented by solicitors, a copy of the questions should, at the same time, be sent to those solicitors.

18.5.1 Further detail on questions

Note Rule 35.6:

1   A party may put to:

   (a) an expert instructed by another party, or

   (b) a single joint expert appointed under Rule 35.7, written questions about his report.

2   Written questions under paragraph (1) –

   (a) may be put once only;

   (b) must be put within 28 days of service of the expert's report; and

   (c) must be for the purpose only of clarification of the report;

unless in any case –

   (i) the court gives permission; or

   (ii) the other party agrees.

(3) An expert's answers to questions put in accordance with paragraph (1) shall be treated as part of the expert's report.

(4) Where –

   (a) a party has put a written question to an expert instructed by another party in accordance with this rule; and

   (b) the expert does not answer the question,

the court may make one or both of the following orders in relation to the party who instructed the expert –

   (i) that the party may not rely on the evidence of that expert; or

   (ii) that the party may not recover the fees and expenses of that expert from any other party.

18.6 Discussion between experts and agreement of issues

The court may direct discussion between experts so as to identify the issues and, where possible, reach an agreement, and the court may itself specify the issues which the experts must address when they meet, requiring the experts to prepare a statement after they have met showing those issues on which they agree and those on which they disagree, with a summary of their reasons for disagreeing. Any agreement between the experts does not bind the parties unless the parties themselves expressly agree to be bound by it (rule 35.12).

18.7 Non-disclosure

Non disclosure of an expert's report means that it cannot be relied upon; nor can the party call the expert to give oral evidence. However, rule 35.13 adds 'unless the Court permits'.

18.8 The court's right to appoint assessors

Under rule 35.19, the court has the right to appoint an assessor to assist the court in dealing with a matter in which the assessor has skill and experience. The assessor will take such part in the proceedings as the court directs and may, at the request of the court, prepare a report which can be disclosed to the parties and which they may use at trial.

The costs of the assessor will be determined by the court, and the latter has the power to order any party to deposit a sum of money in court in respect of the assessor's fees. Where the court does so, the assessor will not be appointed until the payment has been made.

18.9 Practical implications

- It was in the area of experts that Lord Woolf was determined to make changes in the light of the proliferation of biased, dilatory and expensive experts. Now, no one can use an expert or subsequently evince oral evidence from the expert without the court's permission.
- Experts are now reminded that their duty is to the court, not to those who pay their fees, and they must sign a statement acknowledging that fact.
- There have been several cases involving the question of expert evidence since the Rules came into effect, and they have made it

clear that the court is prepared to be robust in refusing to consider expert evidence which has not been presented in accordance with the directions of the court.

- In many cases, particularly small and fast track, the courts have shown a preference for a single, joint expert. However, Lord Woolf has made it clear that, in the more complex cases, such as clinical negligence, it might be more appropriate for each side to be allowed to have their own witnesses.

- There is nothing to stop the parties from having their own, non-appointed experts to advise them, including as to the questions to be put to the single joint appointed expert. However, these 'shadow experts' will not be permitted to give evidence, nor are their fees recoverable from the other side.

19 Hearings and Judgment

19.1 Hearings (Part 39)

19.1.1 General

Note the provisions of rule 39.2:

(1) The general rule is that a hearing is to be in public.

(2) The requirement for a hearing to be in public does not require the court to make special arrangements for accommodating members of the public.

(3) A hearing, or any part of it, may be in private if –

    (a) publicity would defeat the object of the hearing;

    (b) it involves matters relating to national security;

    (c) it involves confidential information (including information relating to personal financial matters) and publicity would damage that confidentiality;

    (d) a private hearing is necessary to protect the interests of any child or patient;

    (e) it is a hearing of an application made without notice and it would be unjust to any respondent for there to be a public hearing;

    (f) it involves uncontentious matters arising in the administration of trusts or in the administration of a deceased person's estate; or

    (g) the court considers this to be necessary, in the interests of justice.

(4) The court may order that the identity of any party or witness must not be disclosed if it considers non-disclosure necessary in order to protect the interests of that party or witness.

(RSC Ord 52, in Sched 1, provides that a committal hearing may be in private.)

Practical implications

There is already a suggested issue under Art 6(1) of the European Convention on Human Rights as to whether the layout of district judges' chambers, situated as many of them are in suites behind locked doors, offends the principle of a fair trial as far as access for the public is concerned. It is felt that, provided that the public are aware that access may be gained with assistance from court staff, the principle will not be offended.

As for those cases which are to be held in private, see 39PD1.5:

1.5 The hearings set out below shall in the first instance be listed by the court as hearings in private under rule 39.2(3)(c), namely:

(1) a claim by a mortgagee against one or more individuals for an order for possession of land,

(2) a claim by a landlord against one or more tenants or former tenants for the repossession of a dwelling house based on the non-payment of rent,

(3) an application to suspend a warrant of execution or a warrant of possession or to stay execution where the court is being invited to consider the ability of a party to make payments to another party,

(4) a redetermination under rule 14.13 or an application to vary or suspend the payment of a judgment debt by instalments,

(5) an application for a charging order (including an application to enforce a charging order), garnishee order, attachment of earnings order, administration order, or the appointment of a receiver,

(6) an oral examination,

(7) the determination of an assisted person's liability for costs under regulation 127 of the Civil Legal Aid (General) Regulations 1989,

(8) an application for security for costs under s 726(1) of the Companies Act 1985, and

(9) proceedings brought under the Consumer Credit Act 1974, the Inheritance (Provision for Family and Dependants) Act 1975 or the Protection from Harassment Act 1997,

(10) an application by a trustee or personal representative for directions as to bringing or defending legal proceedings,

(11) any other necessary documents.

Rule 39.2(3)(d) states that a hearing may be in private where it involves the interests of a child or patient. This includes the approval of a compromise or settlement on behalf of a child or patient or an application for the payment of money out of court to such a person. Attention is drawn to para 5.1 of the Practice Direction which supplements Part 27 (relating to the hearing of claims in the small claims track), which provides that the judge may decide to hold a small claim hearing in private if the parties agree or if a ground mentioned in rule 39.2(3) applies. A hearing of a small claim in premises other than the court will not be a hearing in public. Nothing in this Practice Direction prevents a judge from ordering that a hearing taking place in public shall continue in private, or vice versa.

If the court or judge's room in which the proceedings are taking place has a sign on the door indicating that the proceedings are private, members of the public who are not parties to the proceedings will not be admitted unless the court permits. Where there is no such sign on the door of the court or judge's room, members of the public will be admitted, where practicable. The judge may, if he thinks it appropriate, adjourn the proceedings to a larger room or court.

When a hearing takes place in public, members of the public may obtain a transcript of any judgment given or a copy of any order made, subject to payment of the appropriate fee. When a judgment is given or an order is made in private, if any member of the public who is not a party to the proceedings seeks a transcript of the judgment or a copy of the order, he must seek the leave of the judge who gave the judgment or made the order. A judgment or order given or made in private, when drawn up, must have clearly marked in the title:

Before [*title and name of judge*] sitting in Private.

References to hearings being in public or private or in a judge's room contained in the CPR (including the Rules of the Supreme Court and the County Court Rules scheduled to Part 50) and the Practice Directions which supplement them do not restrict any existing rights of audience or confer any new rights of audience in respect of applications or proceedings which, under the rules previously in force, would have been heard in court or in chambers respectively.

19.1.2   Failure to attend trial (rule 39.3)

On failure of a defendant to attend, the claimant may prove his claim and obtain judgment and, if there is a counterclaim, seek to have it struck out. Where the claimant fails to attend, the defendant may prove his counterclaim and, similarly, seek the striking out of the claim.

In cases where neither party attends, the court may strike out the proceedings. This will mean that a party will be left to apply for restoration, and, where appropriate, for any judgment given to be set aside.

19.1.3   Timetables for trial

Details of the power of the court to fix timetables and fix a date for a trial are set out in rule 28.6 in relation to fast track (see above, Chapter 12) and rule 29.8 for multi-track (see above, Chapter 13). The timetable will be fixed in consultation with the parties (rule 39.4).

19.1.4   Trial bundles

Directions for preparation and lodging are likely to be given at listing stage, but the Rules require a bundle to be lodged not more than seven and not less than three days before trial (rule 39.5(2)), though for fast track the directions as given in the Appendix to PD28 state that the trial bundles must be lodged at least seven days before trial. Where there is a trial window, these periods would no doubt be calculated from the start of the window.

It is important to remember that a claimant will need to compile bundles for each of all other parties, and another for use of the witnesses. Originals of documents in the bundle should be available for production (39PD3.3).

Format of bundles

For the format of bundles, see 39PD3.2. Lever-arch files are desirable, otherwise use a ring file. A separate file is convenient for any expert evidence, and different coloured files, where there is more than one expert, should be used.

19.1.5 Settlement before trial

Note 39PD4:

> 4.1 Where:
>
>> (1) an offer to settle a claim is accepted,
>>
>> (2) or a settlement is reached, or
>>
>> (3) a claim is discontinued,
>
> which disposes of the whole of a claim for which a date or 'window' has been fixed for the trial, the parties must ensure that the listing officer for the trial court is notified immediately.
>
> 4.2 If an order is drawn up giving effect to the settlement or discontinuance, a copy of the sealed order should be filed with the listing officer.

19.1.6 Conduct of the trial

Opening speeches, as before, may be dispensed with, whether on fast or multi-track (28PD8.2 and 29PD10.2). As for presentation of witness evidence, see above, Chapter 17. A company can be represented by an authorised employee, provided that the court gives permission (rule 39.6 and see 39PD5.2 and 5.3). Exhibits proved at the trial will be recorded by the court and kept by it until conclusion of the trial, unless otherwise directed (39PD7).

Usually, the evidence will be recorded (39PD6.1) and a copy of any transcript will be available on payment of a charge (39PD6.3).

19.2 Judgments and orders (Part 40)

19.2.1 General

Every judgment or order, including those made at trial, will be drawn up by the court, unless (rule 40.3(1):

- the court orders a party to draw it up;
- a party, with the permission of the court, agrees to draw it up;
- the court dispenses with the need to draw it up; or
- it is a consent order under rule 40.6 (see below).

19.2.2   Service of judgments or orders

Where a judgment or order has been drawn up by a party and is to be served by the court, the party who drew it up must file a copy and sufficient copies for service (rule 40.4). The court may also order a judgment to be served on the party, notwithstanding that he is represented by a solicitor (rule 40.5).

19.2.3   Consent judgments and orders

The court officer may enter and seal an agreed judgment or order if it is basically for payment of an amount of money, delivery up of goods, dismissal of any proceedings or their stay, the stay of enforcement of a judgment, the setting aside of a default judgment, payment out of money which has been paid into court, the discharge from liability of any party, or the payment, assessment or waiver of costs (rule 40.6).

19.2.4   When does a judgment or order take effect?

A judgment or order takes effect from the day when it is given or made, or at such later date as the court may specify (rule 40.7).

19.2.5   Interest on judgments

The interest shall begin to run from the date that judgment is given, unless there is a rule or Practice Direction which makes a different provision, or the court orders otherwise, and this includes ordering interest to begin from a date before the date that judgment was given (rule 40.9).

19.2.6   Time for complying with a judgment or order

If for payment of an amount of money, including costs, compliance is required within 14 days of the date of the judgment or order, unless that specifies a different date for compliance, or any of the rules specify a different date, or the court has stayed the proceedings or judgment.

19.2.7 'Slip' rule

The court may at any time correct an accidental slip or omission in the judgment or order and a party may apply for a correction without notice (rule 40.12).

19.2.8 Judgment on claim and counterclaim

If specified amounts are awarded both to the claimant on his claim and against the claimant on a counterclaim, then whatever may be the balance in favour of the one of the parties may be subject to an order for the net loser to pay the balance, but the court may make a separate order as to costs (rule 40.13).

20 Offers to Settle and Payments into Court (Part 36)

20.1   Definitions

36.2(1) An offer made in accordance with the requirements of this Part is called –

(a) if made by way of a payment into court, 'a Part 36 payment';

(b) otherwise 'a Part 36 offer'.

(Rule 36.3 sets out when an offer has to be made by way of a payment into court.)

(2) The party who makes an offer is the 'offeror'.

(3) The party to whom an offer is made is the 'offeree'.

20.2   General provisions

Offers to settle do not apply to small claims, unless the court orders otherwise (rule 36.2 (5)), but this, of course, only applies after allocation to track.

An *offer* by a defendant to settle a money claim will not have the advantages as set out in Part 36 unless it is accompanied by a Part 36 payment, and such a payment cannot be made until proceedings have started (rule 36.3). However, note costs rule 44.3(4)(c), which provides that, when dealing with the question of costs, the court can take into account an offer made even if it does not comply with the requirements of rule 36.

The *Calderbank* principle (*Calderbank v Calderbank* [1975] 3 All ER 333) used in family cases is extended to civil cases so that a claimant can make an offer to settle (for example, 'I am prepared to accept £X to settle my claim') which will be binding and, if achieved or improved upon at trial, may entitle the claimant to a 'bonus', including indemnity costs and enhanced interest (see below).

There are provisions for offers and payment in respect of claims which have a partial monetary element. Rule 36.4 enables a defendant to a mixed claim to make a payment in respect of the money part and an offer in respect of the non-money part. It provides that the claimant's acceptance of the payment will constitute acceptance also of the offer. Paragraph 8.11 of the Practice Direction to Part 36 states that the converse is also the case – accept the offer on the non-monetary claim and you are deemed to have accepted the payment.

20.3   Form and content of a Part 36 *offer*

A Part 36 payment or offer may be made at any time after the commencement of proceedings, and may be made in appeal proceedings (rule 36.2(4)). The offer must be in writing and must state which part of the claim it relates to and whether any other factors such as a counterclaim and interest have been taken into account (rule 36.5(1)–(3)). An offer can also be made to settle a claim for provisional damages (rule 36.7).

An offer is made when received by the offeree and is accepted when notice of its acceptance is received by the offeror (rule 36.8).

20.4   Notice of a Part 36 *payment*

Similar provisions apply as with a Part 36 offer, but it will of course be accompanied by a payment (rule 36.6). Acceptance is as for offers (above). Both an offer and a payment may be subject to clarification by the offeree (rule 36.9).

The defendant must file:

• the Part 36 payment notice (N242A) and copy for service, if required;

• the payment (usually a cheque, payable to 'Her Majesty's Paymaster General' or, in the Royal Courts of Justice, to 'the Accountant General of the Supreme Court');

• for the Royal Courts of Justice, Form CFO100 with the Court Funds Office (36PD4.1).

All or part of money paid into court by a defendant following an order under rule 3.1(3) or (5) may be treated by him as a Part 36 payment, in which case he must file a Part 36 payment notice (rule 37.2).

20.5 Court to take account of offer made before proceedings (rule 36.10)

The court can take into account an offer to settle made *before proceedings* were begun when making any order for costs (rule 36.10(1)). The offer must have been expressed as being open for 21 days after the date it was made and, in the case of a potential defendant, include an offer to pay the costs of the offeree (rule 36.10(2)).

If the offeror is a defendant to a money claim and proceedings are subsequently commenced, the offeror must make a Part 36 payment not less than the amount of the offer within 14 days after service of the claim form (rule 36.10(3)). Such an offer or payment cannot be accepted without the leave of the court (rule 36.10(4)).

20.6 Defence of tender

A defendant who wishes to rely on the defence of tender before claim must pay into court the amount he says was tendered, or the defence will not be available to him. The defendant may treat such a payment (or part of it) as a Part 36 payment and, if he does so, must file and serve a payment notice (rule 37.3).

20.7 Acceptance of offer or payment

The relevant period for acceptance is at least 21 days before the date of the trial, failing which the court's permission will be required to accept a payment or offer, provided that the parties agree the liability for costs (rules 36.11 and 36.12). Permission is also required where a claim is compromised on behalf of a child or patient (rule 21.10).

In a claim with two or more defendants who are sued jointly or in the alternative, permission will be required unless the above conditions are satisfied and the claimant discontinues his claim against the other defendant(s) who must also give their written consent to the acceptance of the Part 36 payment or offer (rule 36.17(2)). The claimant may continue against other defendants whom the claimant alleges have several liability (rule 36.17(3)).

20.7.1 Procedure

A notice of acceptance (N243) must be filed in court and served on the offeror. The notice must be properly headed, identify the Part 36 payment or offer to which it relates and be signed by the offeree or his legal representative (36PD8.6, 8.7). Presumably, the consent(s) of other defendants, where necessary, should also be filed and referred to in the notice, and copies served.

Where the offer relates to part of the claim, the notice of acceptance may accept the offer and abandon the remainder of the claim (rule 36.13(2)). Otherwise application for permission must be made, to the trial judge if the trial has started, and otherwise by application notice under Part 23 (rules 36.11(2) and 36.12(2)). The court will make an order for costs if it gives permission (rules 36.11(3) and 36.12(3)).

20.8 Costs and other consequences of acceptance

The claimant will be entitled to his costs of the proceedings up to the date of service of the notice of acceptance, with costs payable on the standard basis if not agreed (rule 36.13). Such costs will include any costs attributable to the defendant's counterclaim if the Part 36 payment or offer states that it takes into account the counterclaim (rule 36.13(3)).

The effect of acceptance will be to stay the proceedings (rule 36.15). As to acceptance of an offer/payment by one of several defendants, see rule 36.17. The privilege attached to offers or payments continues to apply, in as much as the trial judge will be kept ignorant of them until all questions of liability and quantum have been decided (rule 36.19(2)). However, this will not apply (rule 36.19(3)):

(a) where the defence of tender before claim has been raised;

(b) where the proceedings have been stayed under rule 36.15 following acceptance of a Part 36 offer or Part 36 payment; or

(c) where:
   (i) the issue of liability has been determined before any assessment of the money claimed; and
   (ii) the fact that there has or has not been a Part 36 payment may be relevant to the question of the costs or the issue of liability.

A claimant's failure to beat a defendant's offer or payment will result in the claimant paying the costs from the last date of possible acceptance (rule 36.20).

20.8.1 The 'bonus'

Where the claimant beats the offer or payment by the defendant, not only will the claimant be entitled to his costs on an *indemnity basis,* but also interest at a rate not exceeding *10% above base rate* on all or part of his claim and costs, unless the court considers it unjust to do so (rule 36.21(1)–(4)). This 'bonus' depends on the claimant having previously made a Part 36 offer (rule 36.1), but the claimant does not have to beat his own offer.

In considering whether or not it would be unjust, the court will take into account all the circumstances, including (rule 36.21(5)):

(a) the terms of any Part 36 offer;

(b) the stage in the proceedings when any Part 36 offer or Part 36 payment was made;

(c) the information available to the parties at the time when the Part 36 offer or Part 36 payment was made; and

(d) the conduct of the parties with regard to the giving or refusing to give information for the purposes of enabling the offer or payment into court to be made or evaluated.

20.9   Deduction of benefits

The deduction of benefits under the Social Security (Recovery of Benefits) Act 1997 is dealt with in rule 36.23: where a payment to a claimant following acceptance of a Part 36 payment would be a recoverable benefit for the purposes of s 1 of the Social Security (Recovery of Benefits) Act 1997, if the offeror has applied for but has not received a certificate of recoverable benefit when he makes the offer, he must make the payment within seven days of receipt of the certificate.

The court will take into account the gross figure in the Part 36 payment notice when considering whether the claimant has bettered or obtained a more advantageous judgment than the Part 36 payment or offer (36PD10.5).

20.10 Payment out of court (rule 36.16)

A request for payment out, following acceptance of a Part 36 offer, is made on Practice Form N243 (36PD8.1). This contains various details to be completed (see 36PD8.2). Where the request is made to the Royal Courts of Justice, Form CFO201 will also be required (36PD8.3).

Instead of payment to a bank account, the payee can ask for a cheque (36PD8.4). As to payment out to a person who has died intestate, see 36PD8.5.

20.11 Practical implications

- There is little doubt that Part 36 is encouraging parties to make more reasonable proposals to settle disputes resulting in more settlements. The 'bonus' available to claimants has proved an effective incentive to them to put such offers forward.

- However, the wide discretion given to courts by Part 44 as to the award of costs means that, even if an offer is not Part 36 compliant, the court may take it into account. It also means that the court can take into account such matters as the fact that the claimant has failed to beat his own offer and any offers made pre-issue.

21 Costs

21.1 General

The Costs Rules are contained in Parts 43–48 of the CPR. Note rule 44.13(1):

> Where the court makes an order which does not mention costs no party is entitled to costs in relation to that order.

In-house solicitors can now recover costs (rule 48.6). Costs draftsmen's fees can be included in the 'reasonable costs of preparing and checking the bill' (43PD2.16), although whether a costs draftsman is needed to prepare a summary bill of costs (see below) remains to be seen and there is some doubt as to whether such fees can be claimed in detailed assessments of funding assisted family proceedings costs. A solicitor representing himself or his firm may recover full costs and is not limited to costs as a litigant in person (48PD1.7).

21.2 Definitions

Note 44PD2.4:

> There are certain costs orders which the court will commonly make in proceedings before trial. The following table sets out the general effect of these orders. The table is not an exhaustive list of the orders which the court may make.

Term	Effect
• Costs • Costs in any event	The party in whose favour the order is made is entitled to the costs in respect of the part of the proceedings to which the order relates, whatever other costs orders are made in the proceedings.

Term	Effect
• Costs in the case • Costs in the application	The party in whose favour the court makes an order for costs at the end of the proceedings is entitled to his costs of the part of the proceedings to which the order relates.
• Costs reserved	The decision about costs is deferred to a later occasion, but if no later order is made the costs will be costs in the case.
• Claimant's/defendant's costs in the case/application	If the party in whose favour the costs order is made is awarded costs at the end of the proceedings, that party is entitled to his costs of the part of the proceedings to which the order relates. If any other party is awarded costs at the end of the proceedings, the party in whose favour the final costs order is made is not liable to pay the costs of any other party in respect of the part of the proceedings to which the order relates.
• Costs thrown away	Where, for example, a judgment or order is set aside, the party in whose favour the costs order is made is entitled to the costs which have been incurred as a consequence. This includes the costs of; (a) preparing for and attending any hearing at which the judgment or order which has been set aside was made; (b) preparing for and attending any hearing to set aside the judgment or order in question; (c) preparing for and attending any hearing at which the court orders the proceedings or the part in question to be adjourned; (d) any steps taken to enforce a judgment or order which has subsequently been set aside.
• Costs of and caused by	Where, for example, the court makes this order on an application to amend a statement of case, the party in whose favour the costs order is made is entitled to the costs of preparing for and attending the application and the costs of any consequential amendment to his own statement of case.

Term	Effect
• Costs here and below	The party in whose favour the costs order is made is entitled not only to his costs in respect of the proceedings in which the court makes the order but also to his costs of the proceedings in any lower court. In the case of an appeal from a Divisional Court, the party is not entitled to any costs incurred in any court below the Divisional Court.
• No order as to costs • Each party to pay his own costs	Each party is to bear his own costs of the part of the proceedings to which the order relates whatever costs order the court makes at the end of the proceedings.

Further definitions are in rule 43.2:

(1) In Parts 44 to 48, unless the context otherwise requires –

    (a) 'costs' includes fees, charges, disbursements, expenses, remuneration, reimbursement allowed to a litigant in person under rule 48.6 and any fee or reward charged by a lay representative for acting on behalf of a party in proceedings allocated to the small claims track;

    (b) 'costs judge' means a taxing master of the Supreme Court;

    (c) 'costs officer' means -

        (i) a costs judge;

        (ii) a district judge; and

        (iii) an authorised court officer;

    (d) 'authorised court officer' means any officer of -

        (i) a county court;

        (ii) a district registry;

        (iii) the Principal Registry of the Family Division; or

        (iv) the Supreme Court Costs Office;

        whom the Lord Chancellor has authorised to assess costs;

    (e) 'fund' includes any estate or property held for the benefit of any person or class of person and any fund to which a trustee or personal representative is entitled in his capacity as such;

    (f) 'receiving party' means a party entitled to be paid costs;

    (g) 'paying party' means a party liable to pay costs;

(h) 'LSC funded client' means an individual who receives services funded by the Legal Services Commission as part of the Community Legal Service within the meaning of Part I of the Access to Justice Act 1999; and

(i) 'fixed costs' means the amounts which are to be allowed in respect of solicitors' charges in the circumstances set out in Part 45.

Other definitions relate to conditional fee agreements (CFAs) (see below).

21.2.1 Meaning of 'summary assessment'

43.3 'Summary assessment' means the procedure by which the court, when making an order about costs, orders payment of a sum of money instead of fixed costs or 'detailed assessment'.

21.2.2 Meaning of detailed assessment

43.4 'Detailed assessment' means the procedure by which the amount of costs is decided by a costs officer in accordance with Part 47.

21.3 Fees of counsel

'Certificates for counsel' are no longer necessary. 44PD2.6 provides a mechanism for a certificate only when the judge feels that the attention of the taxing officer needs to be drawn to it.

21.4 Solicitor's duty to notify client

Under rule 44.2:

(1) Where:

(a) the court makes a costs order against a legally represented party; and

(b) the party is not present when the order is made,

the party's solicitor must notify his client in writing of the costs order no later than 7 days after the solicitor receives notice of the order.

Note 44PD1.2:

Where a solicitor notifies a client of an order under that rule, he must also explain why the order came to be made.

The court can always call for a copy of the letter that the solicitor sends to the client, or make supply of such a letter a condition of a direction (44PD1.3).

21.5 Court's discretion and circumstances to be taken into account when exercising discretion as to costs

The general rule remains that costs should follow the event. However, the effect of the rules (see below) means that this is very much a rebuttable presumption and there may well be detailed arguments on costs, where before the issue of costs may not have been fully argued.

Note rule 44.3:

(1) The court has discretion as to –

    (a) whether costs are payable by one party to another;

    (b) the amount of those costs; and

    (c) when they are to be paid.

(2) If the court decides to make an order about costs –

    (a) the general rule is that the unsuccessful party will be ordered to pay the costs of the successful party; but

    (b) the court may make a different order.

[In other words, the 'winner takes all' principle no longer invariably applies.]

(3) The general rule does not apply to the following proceedings –

    (a) proceedings in the Court of Appeal on an application or appeal made in connection with proceedings in the Family Division; or

    (b) proceedings in the Court of Appeal from a judgment, direction, decision or order given or made in probate proceedings or family proceedings.

(4) In deciding what order (if any) to make about costs, the court must have regard to all the circumstances, including –

    (a) the conduct of all the parties;

    (b) whether a party has succeeded on part of his case, even if he has not been wholly successful; and

    (c) any payment into court or admissible offer to settle made by a party which is drawn to the court's attention (whether or not made in accordance with Part 36).

[Part 36 contains further provisions about how the court's discretion is to be exercised where a payment into court or an offer to settle is made under that Part.]

(5) The conduct of the parties includes –

    (a) conduct before, as well as during, the proceedings, and in particular the extent to which the parties followed any relevant pre-action protocol;

    (b) whether it was reasonable for a party to raise, pursue or contest a particular allegation or issue;

    (c) the manner in which a party has pursued or defended his case or a particular allegation or issue; and

    (d) whether a claimant who has succeeded in his claim, in whole or in part, exaggerated his claim.

(6) The orders which the court may make under this rule include an order that a party must pay-

    (a) a proportion of another party's costs;

    (b) a stated amount in respect of another party's costs;

    (c) costs from or until a certain date only;

    (d) costs incurred before proceedings have begun;

    (e) costs relating to particular steps taken in the proceedings;

    (f) costs relating only to a distinct part of the proceedings; and

    (g) interest on costs from or until a certain date, including a date before judgment.

(7) Where the court would otherwise consider making an order under paragraph (6)(e), it must instead, if practicable, make an order under paragraph (6)(a) or (c).

(8) Where the court has ordered a party to pay costs, it may order an amount to be paid on account before the costs are assessed.

21.5.1 Practical implications

Practitioners should note that the fact that the receiving party has won does not necessarily mean that they should get all their costs. Arguments may be raised that, for example, the receiving party raised several claims but only succeeded in some of them; that they recovered significantly less than they claimed; or that they misconducted the proceedings. Success with these arguments may mean the receiving party getting less than full costs or, in extreme cases, no costs at all.

21.6   Misconduct

The court may deal with misconduct by a party or his legal representative either in connection with a detailed assessment or with regard to proceedings under rule 44.14.

The court may disallow all or part of the costs which are being assessed; or order the party at fault or his legal representative to pay costs which he has caused any other party to incur (rule 44.14(2)). Note the requirement for a solicitor to notify his client of any costs order made against the client (rule 44.14(3) and see rule 44.2, mentioned above).

Note 44PD7:

7.1 Before making an order under rule 44.14 the court must give the party or legal representative in question a reasonable opportunity to attend a hearing to give reasons why it should not make such an order.

7.2 Conduct before or during the proceedings which gave rise to the assessment which is unreasonable or improper includes steps which are calculated to prevent or inhibit the court from furthering the overriding objective.

7.3 Although rule 44.14(3) does not specify any sanction for breach of the obligation imposed by the rule the court may, either in the order under paragraph (2) or in a subsequent order, require the solicitor to produce to the court evidence that he took reasonable steps to comply with the obligation.

As to wasted costs generally, see rule 48.7:

(1) This rule applies where the court is considering whether to make an order under s 51(6) of the Supreme Court Act 1981 (court's power to disallow or (as the case may be) order a legal representative to meet, 'wasted costs').

(2) The court must give the legal representative a reasonable opportunity to attend a hearing to give reasons why it should not make such an order.

(3) For the purposes of this rule, the court may direct that privileged documents are to be disclosed to the court and, if the court so directs, to the other party to the application for an order.

(4) When the court makes a wasted costs order, it must specify the amount to be disallowed or paid.

(5) The court may direct that notice must be given to the legal representative's client, in such manner as the court may direct –

(a) of any proceedings under this rule; or

(b) of any order made under it against his legal representative.

(6) Before making a wasted costs order, the court may direct a costs judge or a district judge to inquire into the matter and report to the court.

(7) The court may refer the question of wasted costs to a costs judge or a district judge, instead of making a wasted costs order.

The Practice Direction sets out further details of the procedure to be followed.

21.6.1 Practical implications

One of the considerations for relief from sanctions set out in rule 3.9 (see above, Chapter 10) is whether the original default was caused by a litigant or his solicitor. Where it was clearly caused by the solicitor, for example, by missing a date, turning up late at court, etc, the court may not feel that a detailed enquiry is necessary and will make a wasted costs order on the spot. Often, the solicitor will concede that the fault was his and not that of his client.

21.7 Basis of assessment

As previously, there will be two bases of assessment, set out in rule 44.4:

(1) Where the court is to assess the amount of costs (whether by summary or detailed assessment) it will assess those costs –

(a) on the standard basis; or

(b) on the indemnity basis,

but the court will not in either case allow costs which have been unreasonably incurred or are unreasonable in amount.

[Rule 48.3 sets out how the court decides the amount of costs payable under a contract.]

(2) Where the amount of costs is to be assessed on the standard basis, the court will –

(a) only allow costs which are proportionate to the matters in issue; and

(b) resolve any doubt which it may have as to whether costs were reasonably incurred or reasonable and proportionate in amount in favour of the paying party.

(3) Where the amount of costs is to be assessed on the indemnity basis, the court will resolve any doubt which it may have as to whether costs were reasonably incurred or were reasonable in amount in favour of the receiving party.

(4) Where –

(a) the court makes an order about costs without indicating the basis on which the costs are to be assessed; or

(b) the court makes an order for costs to be assessed on a basis other than the standard basis or the indemnity basis, the costs will be assessed on the standard basis.

(5) This rule and Part 47 (detailed assessment of costs by a costs officer) do not apply to the extent that regulations made under the Legal Aid Act 1988 determine the amount payable.

(6) Where the amount of a solicitor's remuneration in respect of non-contentious business is regulated by any general orders made under the Solicitors Act 1974, the amount of the costs to be allowed in respect of any such business which falls to be assessed by the court will be decided in accordance with those general orders rather than this rule and rule 44.5.

The difference between standard and indemnity basis is of vital importance. The burden of proof alters between the two: for standard, it lies with the receiving party; for indemnity, it lies with the paying party. Proportionality is only applied to the standard basis.

21.8 Proportionality in relation to costs

The receiving party will only be entitled to recover the costs which are proportionate – to quote rule 44.4(2)(a) – 'to the matters in issue'. Therefore, the spectacle of costs considerably exceeding the amount recovered is likely to be extremely rare.

In this regard, it is worth considering PD11.1–11.3 to rule 44:

11.1 The relationship between the total of the costs incurred and the financial value of the claim may *not* be a reliable guide. A fixed percentage cannot be applied in *all* cases to the value of the claim in order to ascertain whether or not the costs are proportionate.

11.2 In any proceedings there will be costs which will inevitably be incurred and which are necessary for the successful conduct of the case. Solicitors are not required to conduct litigation at rates which are uneconomic. Thus in a modest claim the proportion of costs is likely to be higher than in a large claim and may even equal or possibly exceed the amount in dispute.

11.3 Where a trial takes place, the time taken by the court in dealing with a particular issue may not be an accurate guide to the amount of time properly spent by the legal or other representatives in preparation for the trial of that issue.

21.8.1 Practical implications

Nowhere does proportionality feature larger in the rules than in relation to costs. The courts have already expressed the view that costs should not be seen to outweigh the value of the claim, although it is recognised that some claims are likely to be more complex than others. As a very rough guide, on a medium size case, say, one falling within the fast track limits of £5,000–£15,000, a useful starting point might be that the costs should not exceed half the value of the claim, the proportion increasing as the value gets lower and decreasing as it gets higher.

21.9 Factors to be taken into account in deciding the amount of costs

The factors are:

44.5(1) The court is to have regard to all the circumstances in deciding whether costs were –

(a) if it is assessing costs on the standard basis –

(i) proportionately and reasonably incurred; or

(ii) were proportionate and reasonable in amount, or

(b) if it is assessing costs on the indemnity basis –

(i) unreasonably incurred; or

(ii) unreasonable in amount.

(2) In particular the court must give effect to any orders which have already been made.

(3) The court must also have regard to –

(a) the conduct of all the parties, including in particular –

(i) conduct before, as well as during, the proceedings; and

(ii) the efforts made, if any, before and during the proceedings in order to try to resolve the dispute;

(b) the amount or value of any money or property involved;

(c) the importance of the matter to all the parties;

(d) the particular complexity of the matter or the difficulty or novelty of the questions raised;

(e) the skill, effort, specialised knowledge and responsibility involved;

(f) the time spent on the case; and

(g) the place where and the circumstances in which work or any part of it was done.

21.10 Fixed costs

In the circumstances set out in rule 45, a party may recover the fixed costs specified in that rule (but the court may make a different order). Details of the amounts of costs are set out in the rule. It is worth noting rule 45.3 as to the liability of the defendant for fixed commencement costs:

(1) Where –

(a) the only claim is for a specified sum of money; and

(b) the defendant pays the money claimed within 14 days after service of particulars of claim on him, together with the fixed commencement costs stated in the claim form,

the defendant is not liable for any further costs unless the court orders otherwise.

(2) Where – ...

(d) the claimant gives notice of acceptance of a payment into court in satisfaction of the whole claim;

(e) the only claim is for a specified sum of money; and

(f) the defendant made the payment into court within 14 days after service of the particulars of claim on him, together with the fixed costs stated in the claim form,

the defendant is not liable for any further costs unless the court orders otherwise.

21.11 Procedure for assessing costs

The assessment procedure is itself subject to quite substantial change, although much of this reflects recent previous practice. Under rule 44.7:

(1) Where the court orders a party to pay costs to another party (other than fixed costs) it may either:

    (a) make a summary assessment of the costs; or

    (b) order detailed assessment of the costs by a costs officer,

unless any rule, practice direction or other enactment provides otherwise.

21.11.2 Summary assessment

The court has power to summarily assess costs at any hearing where it does not order fixed costs, or where fixed costs are not provided for (44PD4.1). The courts will use this power as often as possible where an *inter partes* costs order is made. It will not be appropriate where costs are reserved or where the order is *costs in the case* (formerly 'costs in the cause') or where the receiving party is an assisted person or Legal Services Commission funded client (44PD13.9) or a child or patient, unless the right to claim further costs has been waived (44PD13.11).

Summary assessment is most likely to take place in the county court in relation to fast track hearings, interim or other hearings which do not last longer than a day, unless there is some other good reason for summary assessment not to take place (44PD13.2). The fact that there is a CFA in existence will not, by itself, be a good reason for a summary assessment not to take place (44PD13.3).

Note carefully 44PD13.5:

(1) It is the duty of the parties and their legal representatives to assist the judge in making a summary assessment of costs in any case to which para 13.2 applies, in accordance with the following paragraphs.

(2) Each party who intends to claim costs must prepare a written statement of the costs he intends to claim showing separately in the form of a schedule:

    (a) the number of hours to be claimed;

    (b) the hourly rate to be claimed;

    (c) the grade of fee earner;

    (d) the amount and nature of any disbursement to be claimed, other than counsel's fee for appearing at the hearing;

    (e) the amount of solicitor's costs to be claimed for attending or appearing at the hearing;

    (f) the fees of counsel to be claimed in respect of the hearing; and

    (g) any Value Added Tax to be claimed on these amounts.

(3) The statement of costs should follow as closely as possible Form N260 and must be signed by the party or his legal representative. Where a litigant is an assisted person or is a LSC funded client or is represented by a solicitor in the litigant's employment the statement of costs need not include the certificate appended at the end of Form N260.

(4) The statement of costs must be filed at court and copies of it must be served on any party against whom an order for payment of those costs is intended to be sought. The statement of costs should be filed and the copies of it should be served as soon as possible and in any event not less than 24 hours before the date fixed for the hearing.

(5) Where the litigant is or may be entitled to an additional liability the statement filed and served need not reveal the amount of that liability.

Failure to comply with above provisions may be taken into account by the court when considering the costs of the hearing or assessment (44PD13.6). The figure for assessed costs pronounced by the court will be totally inclusive of all charges (44PD 13.7).

In a case involving an 'additional liability', such as a success fee in a CFA case (see below, 21.16), the assessment of the base costs can take place at an interim hearing, but any assessment of the additional liability will have to wait until the end of the case (44PD13.12). As to the procedure for assessment where there is an additional liability, see 44PD14 and below, 21.11.8.

21.11.3 Proportionality

The fact that there is no dispute from the paying party to an amount claimed for summary assessment does not prevent the court from scrutinising the amount and disallowing such sums as are clearly disproportionate (44PD13.13(a)).

21.11.4 Practical implications

- Summary assessment has already proved itself to be extremely popular. Although the assessment may be somewhat 'rough and ready', it nevertheless provides for an instant valuation, which also means a quick recovery of costs which, unless the court orders otherwise, must be paid within 14 days of the order for payment.

- It must be borne in mind that, in assessing costs, the court will be applying proportionality. Thus, even if all steps taken for a particular application were reasonable and were reasonably charged, if the total is disproportionate either for that kind of application or in relation to the overall claim, the court is likely to reduce it.

- Practitioners are advised to prepare, serve and file a schedule for summary assessment for every interim hearing, even if they are not expecting to recover costs, as it may well be that, on the day, it suddenly appears they are entitled to them, for example, on a case management conference where the other side does not turn up.

- Failure to prepare and serve a schedule is likely to result in only nominal costs or no costs at all being awarded.

- The advent of benchmark costs, whereby recommended costs will be allowable for different types of application, which are at present being considered by the Supreme Court Costs Office, may well see a decrease in the incidence of summary assessment.

21.11.5 Detailed assessment

The detailed assessment which replaces the previous taxation procedure is much as before, save in one general important respect. There is at least now one specific burden on the paying party, namely, they must now positively object to costs, failing which *all* the costs will be assessed as claimed by the receiving party. This is set out in Section II of Part 47.

The Practice Direction to Part 47 sets out full details for drawing up a bill for detailed assessment. There are four new forms of bill, with single columns for profit costs disbursements and VAT, together with columns for 'LSC only' items. There is no 'taxed off' column. There is another form for use where a CFA is in existence to allow for success fees and insurance premiums to be claimed.

The new forms are supposed to be computer-friendly, and a disk copy must be provided free of charge to the other party if a computerised form is used. Note that the bill should not contain costs which have been previously summarily assessed (see above).

What was called the A+B basis for assessing costs has now gone; that is, 'care and conduct' are now included in the rates claimed. The assessment procedure is now based on a straight hourly charge, which includes the uplift for care and conduct. Guideline hourly rates are published by the Supreme Court Costs Office. The bill will have to be submitted by the receiving party within three months after the date of the order for payment (rule 47.7). The Rules set out sanctions for failure to submit the bill in time, that is, that interest will not be allowed on the costs for any period over and above the three months (rule 47.8(3)).

Further, the paying party can force the pace by making application to court that the receiving party start the assessment, failing which the costs will be totally disallowed (rule 47.8(1) and (2)).

Having received the bill, the paying party must, within 21 days, serve points of dispute of service of the bill (rule 47.9(2)). A computer-friendly form for points of dispute is set out in the Practice Direction. The receiving party may serve a reply within a further 21 days.

21.11.6 Default costs certificate

If no points of dispute are served, the receiving party can apply to court for a default costs certificate (rule 47.9(4)). However, even if points of dispute are served late, this will prevent any default costs certificate from being issued (rule 47.9(5)). It will also mean that the paying party may not be heard on the detailed assessment without the court's permission. Provision is made for the setting aside of a default costs certificate if a party was not entitled to it (rule 47.12).

21.11.7 Interim costs certificate

At any time after having filed a request for detailed assessment, the receiving party may apply to the court for an interim costs certificate (rule 47.15). This entitles the receiving party to receive, effectively on account, the amount stated on the certificate. The application is made using the Part 23 procedure (see above, Chapter 15), and will be used to seek payment for those items in the detailed bill where points in dispute are not raised.

Subject to having served the bill, the notice of commencement of the assessment procedure and any points of dispute, the receiving party must apply for a hearing (on Form 258A) within three months of the commencement of the detailed assessment proceedings (rule 47.14). When applying for the hearing, the receiving party must file with Form 258A the various documents set out in 47PD39.2. Only items included in the points of dispute can be debated, unless the court gives permission to the contrary (rule 47.14(7)).

When the detailed assessment is completed, a bill will be lodged with the balance of the taxing fee and a certificate will be forthcoming, which can then be enforced (rule 47.16).

21.11.8 Assessing any additional liability

A success fee under a CFA (see below) or an insurance premium paid to fund litigation may be claimed against the losing party. It is a precondition of this that notice of such a fee (but not the amount) must first be served on the other party (rule 44.15) in Form N251 (for procedure, see 44.15PD19). For sanctions for failure to serve such a notice and relief therefrom, see rule 3 (above, Chapter 10).

Assessment of the additional liability does not take place until after the final hearing (rule 44.3A) and may be on a summary or detailed basis (see above). The court will first assess the base costs in the usual way (see above) and then go on to assess the additional liability (44PD11.5). It will consider the factors in the light of the circumstances which existed at the time that the funding arrangement was entered into (44PD11.7). The factors include (44PD11.8(1)):

(a) the risk that the circumstances in which the costs, fees or expenses would be payable might or might not occur;

(c) the legal representative's liability for disbursements;

(d) what other methods of financing were available to the receiving party.

Disproportionality alone will not be a ground for reducing the rate (44PD11.9). When assessing the costs of insurance cover, the court will look at alternative cover available for extent and cost (44PD11.10).

21.11.9 Practical implications

The assessment of an additional liability may be somewhat complicated for judges, for many of whom CFAs are a completely new concept. Practitioners should therefore be prepared to help the court in this regard.

21.12 Legal aid and LSC funding

21.12.1 Definitions

The Legal Services Commission (LSC) replaced the Legal Aid Board in April 2000. All references to 'legal aid' in the new Rules and Practice Directions have been removed. A legally aided litigant becomes 'an assisted person', while a party who obtains LSC funding is an 'LSC funded client'. The fund out of which costs for such persons are paid is the Community Legal Services Fund. Such costs are assessed on the standard basis (see above), with proportionality applying.

The costs of the assessment procedure will fall in the usual way. '*Calderbank*' offers to settle can be made and may have the usual costs effect, even where no required payment into court has been made (rule 47.19). However, such offers will not be taken into account where the receiving party is assisted or LSC funded, unless the court so orders (47PD7.6).

An application for costs against an assisted or LSC funded person, or the LSC itself, is made to the relevant district or costs judge, who, instead of a detailed assessment, carries out a determination of 'full costs' (rule 44.17). For procedure, see 44PD21–23.

21.13 Litigants in person

The appropriate rule is 48.6. For the purposes of this rule, a litigant in person includes (rule 48.6(6)):

(a) a company or other corporation which is acting without a legal representative; and

(b) a barrister, solicitor, solicitor's employee or other authorised litigator (as defined in the Courts and Legal Services Act 1990) who is acting for himself.

The costs recoverable by a litigant in person must not exceed, except in the case of a disbursement, two-thirds of the amount which would have been allowed if the litigant in person had been represented by a legal representative (rule 48.6(2)).

A litigant in person may recover (rule 48.6(3)):

(a) such costs which would have been allowed if the work had been done or the disbursements made by a legal representative on the litigant in person's behalf;

(b) the payments reasonably made by him for legal services relating to the conduct of the proceedings; and

(c) the costs of obtaining expert assistance in connection with assessing the claim for costs.

Subject to the two-thirds rule in rule 48.6 (above), unless the litigant in person is able to prove financial loss (as to which see 48.6PD1.7), the amount of costs which shall be allowed to him for any item of work shall relate to the time reasonably spent by him doing the work (rule

48.6(4)). By 48.6PD1.9, the amount which may be allowed to a litigant in person under rules 46.3(5)(b) and 48.6(4) is £9.25 per hour. A litigant in person who recovers costs for his own attendance at court cannot, in addition, claim a witness allowance for himself (rule 48.6(5)).

21.14 Costs payable under a contract

48.3(1) Where the court assesses (whether by the summary or detailed procedure) costs which are payable by the paying party to the receiving party under the terms of a contract, the costs payable under those terms are, unless the contract expressly provides otherwise, to be presumed to be costs which –

(a) have been reasonably incurred; and

(b) are reasonable in amount,

and the court will assess them accordingly.

(2) This rule does not apply where the contract is between a solicitor and his client.

As to the assessment, 48.3PD50.1 provides that the court may make an order that all or part of the costs payable under the contract shall be disallowed if the court is satisfied by the paying party that costs have been unreasonably incurred or are unreasonable in amount.

As to costs relating to a mortgage, see 48.3PD50.3. Basically, the mortgagee retains his right to costs pursuant to contract. By 48.3PD50.4, a mortgagor may require the mortgagee to provide an account of those costs and dispute them.

21.15 Group litigation order

As to costs, see rule 48.6.

21.16 Conditional fee agreements (rule 48.9)

Where a client seeks taxation of his solicitor's bill rendered under a conditional fee agreement, either or both of the base cost and the conditional uplift will be subject to assessment on the indemnity basis. See the Practice Direction to rule 48.9:

2.16 The factors relevant to assessing the percentage increase include:

(a) the risk that the circumstances in which the fees or expenses would be payable might not occur;

(b) the disadvantages relating to the absence of payment on account;

(c) whether the amount which might be payable under the conditional fee agreement is limited to a certain proportion of any damages recovered by the client;

(d) whether there is a conditional fee agreement between the solicitor and counsel;

(e) the solicitor's liability for disbursements.

When the court is considering the factors to be taken into account, it will have regard to the circumstances as they reasonably appeared to the solicitor or counsel when the conditional fee agreement was entered into or at the time of any variation of the agreement.

21.17 Small claims costs and fast track costs

Fixed costs for small claims and fast track are regulated by rule 44.9:

(1) Part 27 (Small claims) and [the fast track costs rules] contain special rules about:

(a) liability for costs;

(b) the amount of costs which the court may award; and

(c) the procedure for assessing costs.

(2) Those special rules do not apply until a claim is allocated to a particular track.

This needs to be read in conjunction with the main rules, that is, Parts 27 and 28. The general rule for small claims is that there will be no costs awarded save for the limited costs specified in the Rules and Practice Directions. (see above, Chapter 11).

In fast track cases, there are fixed costs for trial. The recoverable trial costs for the advocate will range between £350 and £750, depending on the size of the claim (that is, the resulting judgment), not the length of the trial. The claimant's advocate's costs will depend on the amount recovered, the defendant's on the amount claimed. An attendance of £250 for an accompanying solicitor may be allowed, but only in particular circumstances. Note that if a fast track trial has to go over from the one day allotted to it, no refresher fee is payable.

21.18 Costs only litigation

Where parties have agreed all issues except for costs, rule 44.12A and the Practice Direction thereto (44.12APD17) set out the procedure to be followed. Where proceedings have not been started, a Part 8 application (see above, Chapter 5) for a detailed assessment is issued, provided that there has been a written agreement to pay costs. The dispute may be heard by a costs or district judge or an authorised court officer with the consent of the parties (44.12APD17.5).

If the defendant files an acknowledgment of service disputing the proceedings, they will be dismissed (44.12APD17.9).

21.19 Court fees

Details of these may be found in the County Court Fees Order 1999 (SI 1999/689) and Supreme Court Fees Order 1980 (SI 1980/821), and amendments thereto. For details, see below, Chapter 24.

As for exemptions, reductions or remissions of fees in the county court, note the following parts of the County Court Fees Order:

5(1)   No fee shall be payable under this Order by a party who, at the time when a fee would otherwise become payable:

(a)   is in receipt of any qualifying benefit, and

(b)   is not in receipt of representation under Part IV of the Legal Aid Act 1988 for the purposes of the proceedings.

(2)   The following are qualifying benefits for the purposes of paragraph (1)(a) above –

(a)   income support;

(b)   family credit and disability working allowance under Part VII of the Social Security Contributions and Benefits Act 1992; and

(c)   income-based jobseeker's allowance under the Jobseekers Act 1995.

(3)   Paragraph (1) shall not apply to fee 4.8 (fee payable on a consolidated attachment of earnings order or an administration order).

6   Where it appears to the Lord Chancellor that the payment of any fee prescribed by this Order would, owing to the exceptional circumstances of the particular case, involve undue financial hardship, he may reduce or remit the fee in that case.

21.20 Appeals in assessment proceedings

For an appeal from an assessment by a judge, see below, Chapter 22. Appeals from an authorised court officer relate to High Court matters and are outside the scope of this book. For details, see rule 47.20–23.

21.21 Costs estimates

At certain stages in proceedings, namely, with the filing of the allocation and listing questionnaires, or if the court orders, the parties have to give estimates of costs. 44PD6 deals with form of such estimates and the procedure for supplying them. The direction does not apply to small claims.

In a case where an additional liability, such as a CFA (see above) applies, the estimate need only contain the 'base costs' and not the amount of the additional liability (44PD6.2). A form of estimate is provided in the Schedule to the Costs Precedents, in Form H (44PD6.5), a copy of which is reproduced below, Chapter 24. Practitioners should be aware that the court, when assessing costs, may have regard to the estimates they have given (44PD6.6).

21.22 Practical implications

- The costs rules beg the question of pitching the right level of costs. It might be thought that there may be a temptation to overestimate costs 'just in case'. The problem with this is that, first, the court could scrutinise the estimate as soon as it sees it and suggest a ceiling on costs if it would appear that they will get out of hand or are disproportionate. Secondly, at the end of the day, if costs come in at somewhat less than the estimate, the winning party will be open to challenge that the overestimate was deliberate and amounts to misconduct and, therefore, the actual costs should be reduced accordingly. The client, too, is not going to be happy about being told that the *inter partes* costs he is getting are much less than estimated.
- Underestimates also contain clear dangers. They could be regarded as misleading by the court, paying party and the client, to the extent that practitioners may be held to them.
- It is now apparent that practitioners will have to strive to pitch the estimate at about the right level or suffer consequences later on.

22 Appeals (Part 52)

22.1 General

The rules as to appeals in Part 52 do not apply to an appeal against a
detailed assessment of costs by an authorised court officer (rule 52.1(2)).
The appeals procedure *does* apply to all other orders made by judges,
including those against summary or detailed assessment of costs (see
above, Chapter 21). As from 2 October 2000, the rules also apply to
small claims hearings.

With very few exceptions, permission is now required to appeal
from a decision of a county court judge (rule 52.3). The application
for permission may be made either to the court who made the decision
or to the appeal court in an appeal notice (rule 52.3(2)). The court may
decide the application without a hearing (52PD4.11–14) or at a hearing
(52PD4.15–16).

Unless the court orders otherwise, the notice of appeal must be filed
no later than 14 days from the date of the decision appealed against (rule
52.4(2)). The lodging of the appeal does not automatically operate as
a stay on the order of the lower court (rule 52.7).

For details of the procedure to be followed and the documents
required on an appeal, see the Practice Direction. Note that, on the
appeal, unless the court orders otherwise, no oral evidence or evidence
which was not before the lower court will be allowed (rule 52.11(2)).

22.2 Grounds for appeal

22.2.1 Permission

Permission to appeal will only be granted where the court feels that the
appeal stands a reasonable prospect of success or there is some other
compelling reason for the appeal to go ahead (rule 52.3(6)).

22.2.2   Allowing an appeal

The appellate court will allow an appeal where it considers that the decision of the lower court was wrong or unjust because of a serious procedural or other irregularity (rule 52.11(3)). Any grounds in the notice should therefore be stated as falling within one or both of those categories (52PD3.2).

22.2.3   Appeal from a case management decision

Note 52PD4.5:

> Where the application is for permission to appeal from a case management decision, the court dealing with the application may take into account whether:
>
> (1) the issue is of sufficient significance to justify the costs of an appeal;
>
> (2) the procedural consequences of an appeal (eg loss of trial date) outweigh the significance of the case management decision;
>
> (3) it would be more convenient to determine the issue at or after trial.

22.3   Routes of appeal

52PD2A.1 sets out the usual routes of appeal. Decisions of district judges go to the circuit judge; decisions of the circuit judge go to a High Court judge and thereafter to the Court of Appeal. However, where the decision is one made at the final hearing of a multi-track case or in specialist proceedings (see rule 49(2)), then appeal is made straight to the Court of Appeal.

22.4   Practical implications

- The harmonisation of the procedures for appeal throughout the civil structure is to be welcomed.

- The substitution of the limited grounds of appeal in small claims matters with similar procedures, as for other appeals, probably owes as much to the ramifications of the Human Rights Act 1998 as to any desire to be consistent.

- The interpolation of the requirement to request permission for appeal, requiring as it does the standard of a reasonable prospect of success with the appeal itself, ought to act as a sensible barrier to unmeritorious appeals. However, the ground for appeal that 'the judge got it wrong' may be seen as a little too simplistic.

23 Enforcement

23.1 General

The main provisions governing enforcement fall under CCR Ord 25, which was not affected by the introduction of the CPR 1998. There are various forms of enforcement, and it is for the judgment creditor ('the creditor') to decide which is the appropriate one to use.

Applications for oral examination, charging orders, attachment of earnings or a judgment summons should be dealt with by the county court appropriate to the address of the debtor or his/her place of business. The creditor will, therefore, have to ask, without notice, for the papers to be transferred to the appropriate court for enforcement if it is not the court where judgment was obtained (CCR 25 r.2(1)). Where a case is required to be transferred from one county court to another for enforcement, the order for transfer may be made by a proper officer (Ord 25 r 2(2)).

A county court judgment for £2,000 or more may be transferred to the High Court for enforcement (see below)).

In general, the claimant can choose whether to enforce his court judgment in the county court or the High Court. However, if he seeks to enforce wholly or partly by execution against goods, then Art 8 of the High Court and County Court Jurisdiction Order 1991 (SI 1991/724), as amended, provides that:

- the High Court has exclusive enforcement jurisdiction where the sum which it is sought to enforce under a county court judgment is £5,000 or more and the judgment did not arise out of an agreement regulated under the Consumer Credit Act 1974; and

- the county court has exclusive enforcement jurisdiction over a county court judgment where (a) the sum is less than £2,000, and (b) the judgment arose out of a regulated Consumer Credit Act agreement.

23.2   Enforcement of High Court judgments and orders

High Court judgments and orders, and also judgments, orders, decrees and awards of other courts or awards of an arbitrator which are enforceable as if they were judgments of the High Court, may be enforced in the appropriate county court, usually that in whose district the debtor resides or carries on business. A transfer of the proceedings under s 40 of the County Courts Act 1984 is not required for enforcement by charging order, attachment of earnings or judgment summons. Order 25 r 11 applies and the judgment creditor shall file in the appropriate court (with such documents as are required for enforcing a judgment or order of a county court, that is, a request for enforcement) the following documents:

• an office copy of the judgment or order or, in the case of a judgment, order, decree or award of a court other than the High Court or an arbitrator such evidence of the judgment, order, decree or award and of its enforceability as a judgment of the High Court as the district judge may require;

• an affidavit confirming the amount due under the judgment, order, decree or award (N321); and

• where a writ of execution has been issued to enforce it, a copy of the sheriff's return to the writ.

There is no fee on the transfer itself, although the appropriate county court fee is payable on any accompanied request for enforcement. Unlike tribunal awards (see below), no order is made by the county court. Once the application has been checked and approved, it will be passed to the appropriate section to deal with any requested form of enforcement.

For enforcement against a firm, Ord 25 r 9 does not apply, but instead RSC Ord 81 r 5 applies (see Ord 29 r 9(5)).

23.3   Enforcement of awards of tribunals

Order 25 r 12 applies. Where, by any Act or statutory instrument other than the County Court Rules, a sum of money may be recoverable as if it were payable under an order of the county court, enforcement in the county court may be ordered (Forms N322 – Order for Recovery of Money Awarded by a Tribunal; N322A – Application for an Order). The requirements are:

• an application in Form N322A, which contains a certificate confirming the amount remaining due;

- the award, order or agreement (or duplicate thereof);
- fee (see below, Chapter 24).

Unless otherwise provided, the application is filed in the court for the district in which the person by whom the sum is payable resides or carries on business. The application is made without notice by filing the documents with fee, and the application is dealt with by a proper officer. The award may be enforced thereafter as if it were a county court judgment.

23.4　Enforcement of county court judgments in the High Court

The procedure is laid down by Ord 22 r 8(1). The requirements are:

- a certificate (N293) should be lodged with the county court; and
- a copy of the application (or order) is attached to the request for a certificate.

If the enforcement is intended to be by way of execution against goods, then the order for transfer can be made by a proper officer on granting the certificate of judgment (rule 8(1)(A)). In all other cases, an application on notice will be necessary. The signed and sealed certificate of judgment, with copy, is then presented to the action department on personal attendance. The certificate is treated for enforcement purposes as a High Court judgment.

The advantage of enforcing in the High Court is that the High Court allows interest on the judgment debt (from the date of issue of the certificate allowing it to be transferred to the High Court). There is no interest on a county court judgment debt under £5,000.

23.5　Oral examination

Under Ord 25 r 3, 'the creditor' may issue against the judgment debtor ('the debtor') or an officer of a debtor company. The person to be orally examined may also be ordered to produce any books or documents relevant to means. The requirements on issue are:

- application (N316);
- plaint note;
- fee (see below, Chapter 24) and travelling expenses (optional);
- self-addressed envelope, if by post.

The order for oral examination is served either by the judgment creditor on the debtor personally or by the court sending it to the debtor by first class post, or on his solicitor if he is on the record (CCR 25, r 3(3)), together with conduct money (travelling expenses), if desired.

The oral examination is usually conducted by an officer of the court. There is no requirement that the creditor must be present. A copy of the statement of means taken either at the examination or supplied by the debtor beforehand is supplied to the creditor, who may accept any proposals made therein to obviate the need for further enforcement. If the debtor fails to attend the examination, the court may fix a further hearing (CCR 25 r 3(4) (Form N39). If the debtor fails to attend an adjourned hearing, he may be liable to committal (N40) (see below, 23.15).

23.5.1 Effectiveness

Although the threat of committal gives teeth to this method of enforcement, the difficulty usually lies with the delay between the issue of the order and the eventual examination of a reluctant debtor. However, once an examination does take place, it may yield valuable information about the debtor to enable further enforcement proceedings to be taken, such as garnishee (see below, 23.11) and charging orders (below, 23.12) or attachment of earnings (below, 23.9).

23.6 Execution against goods

The main provisions for an execution against goods can be found under CCR Ord 26. The requirements on issue are:

- request (N323);
- plaint note;
- fee (see below, Chapter 24);
- self-addressed envelope, if by post.

The warrant (N42) may issue for the whole of the unpaid balance of a money judgment and costs or for overdue and unpaid instalments exceeding at least £50, or one monthly or four weekly instalments, whichever is the greater (CCR 26 r 1(2)). A warrant number will be given and this, together with the plaint number, should be used whenever directing any enquiry to the court concerning the warrant.

23.6.1 Execution against a firm

Where a judgment or order is against a firm, execution may be issued against:

- the property of the firm;
- a person who admits or is adjudged to be a partner;
- any person who was served as a partner where judgment is obtained in default of defence or attendance; or
- any other person found by the district judge to be liable following filing of application on notice by the creditor (Ord 25 r 9(1)(3)).

23.6.2 Levy

The warrant is executed by bailiffs of the court for the district where the goods are situated, and all enquiries concerning execution should be directed there, giving the local warrant number, the plaint number and the home court warrant number. On levy, the bailiff hands a notice of levy to the debtor (N42) or leaves the notice at the place of levy. Unless the goods have already been levied upon, forcible entry is not permitted. If the goods are saleable, the bailiff usually takes 'walking possession', unless payment is likely to be made in a reasonable time, in which case a period is usually allowed for payment.

Any contrary claim against the goods, for example, by a spouse, must be made in writing to the bailiff (Ord 33) (see below, 23.6.4). 'Necessary items' are exempt from execution. These will include such tools, books, vehicles and other items of equipment as are necessary to the debtor for use personally in his or her job or business and such clothing, bedding, furniture, household equipment and provisions as are necessary for satisfying the basic domestic needs of the debtor and his or her family (s 89 of the 1984 Act).

After the removal of the goods, they are eventually sold at an auction and any balance after the deduction of sale fees is paid to the creditor. If there are insufficient goods on which to levy (and this is often the case), a notice to this effect is sent to the creditor or his/her solicitors, who will have to consider an alternative method of enforcement.

23.6.3 Suspension of warrant

Under Ord 25 r 8, a debtor may apply on notice to the court to suspend a warrant of execution, giving grounds for doing so – usually a proposal for payment of the debt by instalments. The application does not of itself operate as a stay unless that is also requested. A creditor may also request suspension of a warrant. A suspended warrant may be re-issued on application by the creditor if any condition to which the suspension was subject has not been complied with.

23.6.4 Claims to goods (interpleader)

Under Ord 33, a contrary claim to goods levied upon must in the first instance be given in writing to the bailiff, stating the grounds. Notice (N358) is then sent to the creditor, who has four days in which to admit or deny the claim. In the absence of a reply, or where the claim is disputed, the district judge will issue an interpleader summons (N88) for hearing on a fixed date before the judge.

23.6.5 Effectiveness

Where the debt is £2,000 or more, it is worth considering transferring the case to the High Court for enforcement (see above, 23.4). Apart from this, many warrants are returned for 'insufficient goods' or are countered by applications to suspend the warrant or even to set aside the judgment. Sometimes, they result in the debtor paying up the debt. The number of occasions when goods are actually seized and sold is smaller in comparison. Sometimes, it is more effective to issue a warrant for one or more missed instalments rather than the whole of the balance.

23.7 Warrants of delivery

There are two types of warrant of delivery (Ord 26 r 16): first, that of 'specific delivery', which applies to cases where a delivery-up is ordered; and, secondly, a warrant of delivery with an alternative of paying the value of the goods. The requirements on issue are as for a warrant of execution (see above, 23.6).

Where, apart from delivery-up, a creditor also has a money judgment, execution for this may take place at the same time (Ord 26 r 16(4)). In hire purchase cases, where goods are already disposed of or sale costs are inadequate to meet debt, the creditor may apply on notice for the order for delivery-up to be revoked and replaced with a money judgment.

Actually finding the goods, in particular where cars are involved, can sometimes be a problem, requiring the creditor to return to court for a money judgment instead.

23.8   Warrant of possession

A judgment or order for the recovery of land may be enforced by a warrant of possession (Ord 26 r 17). The requirements on issue are as follows:

*   request (N325);
*   plaint note;
*   fee (see below, Chapter 24);
*   self-addressed envelope, if by post.

Where, apart from possession, a creditor also has a money judgment, execution for this may take place at the same time on paying a separate fee. The warrant lasts three months and thereafter requires leave to be extended (Ord 24 r 6(2)).

Both parties are given notice of the appointment at which the bailiff will attend at the premises. The creditor or a representative ought to be present to secure the premises after possession has been obtained by, for example, changing the locks. All persons present on the premises must leave (*R v Wandsworth County Court* [1975] 3 All ER 390).

Wrongful re-entry after possession is enforceable in the first instance by a without notice warrant of restitution (N50 or N51), and thereafter by an application for an injunction (Ord 26 r 17(5)). For a suspension of a warrant, applications are made to the district judge.

Creditors must expect a delay between the date the order for possession becomes effective and the date that the bailiffs actually respond to the warrant. In the meantime, debtors can, and often do, make applications to suspend the warrant, sometimes applying more than once.

23.9   Attachment of earnings

Under Ord 27 and the Attachment of Earnings Act 1971, a county court may make an attachment of earnings order to secure payments under a High Court or county court order involving a maintenance order or payments under an administration order. Application is made to the court for the district in which the debtor resides (Ord 27 r 3(1)) so that a transfer may be necessary (Ord 25 r 2(1)(c)).

The requirements on issue are:

*   application (N337);
*   fee (see below, Chapter 24);
*   plaint note;

- self-addressed envelope, if by post.

In addition, where judgment is of a court other than a county court:

- office copy judgment; and
- an affidavit verifying the amount due (N321).

If a High Court judgment, an office copy of sheriff's return (Ord 25 r 11) is required.

The name and address of the debtor's employer, if known, should also be stated in the application. In addition, the creditor may indicate on the application form that s/he wishes the court to deal with all the steps in the application in his/her absence (which is often the case).

Notice of the application (N55) is served on the debtor, with a form of reply (N56) on which the debtor endorses details of his/her financial position. Service of the documents is usually effected by the court by post, unless otherwise provided for (for example, N58), unless the creditor wishes to serve, in which case an affidavit of service will be required.

23.9.1 Time for service and reply

Notice of the application (N55) is served on the debtor and must be effected at least 21 days before the return date, or 28 days if by post. Unless the debtor pays the balance owing, s/he must file the form of reply (N56) no more than eight days from the date of service. The court sends a copy of the reply to the creditor (Ord 27 r 5(3)). If the debtor does not reply in time and the judgment creditor knows the employer, the court (proper officer) should be asked by letter to request the employer (N338) to give details of earnings (Ord 27 r 6).

Where a reply is filed by a debtor in compliance with Ord 27 r 5(2) within eight days, and he gives the name and address of his employer, the proper officer can still send notice (N338) to the employer requesting him to file a statement of earnings (Ord 27 r 6). Such a notice may be sent to an employer if the debtor gives information as to his earnings but the court doubts the debtor's statement.

If an employer does not send a statement of earnings in compliance with the request, the court may compel him to do so (ss 14(1)(b), 23(2)(c) of the Attachment of Earnings Act 1971; see Ord 27 r 15 as to enforcement) (N61A). If he has sufficient information to do so, the proper officer will make an order on receipt of the form, sending a copy to the parties and to the employer (Ord 27 r 7(1)). If the debtor fails to pay or to return the form, the proper officer will order him to file a statement of means in Form N61. Failure to reply will then result in the issue of a notice to show cause, which will be listed before the district judge (Ord 27 r 7(A)).

Order 27 r 19 provides for an application for a consolidated order to be made in any proceedings in which an attachment of earnings order (except a priority order) is in force. Order 27 r 19(4) enables the proper officer to make a consolidated attachment of earnings order where a further attachment of earnings order is applied for (see below).

The judgment creditor or the debtor may, within 14 days of service of the order on him and giving his reasons, apply on notice for the order to be reconsidered, and the proper officer shall fix a day for the hearing of the application and give to the judgment creditor and the debtor not less than two days' notice of the day so fixed (Ord 27 r 7(2)). The district judge may confirm the order or set it aside and make such new order as he thinks fit, or, instead, a day may be fixed for hearing by the district judge (Ord 27 r 7(5)).

Where on a hearing before a district judge the debtor fails to attend, if the district judge feels that an adjourned hearing is necessary, he will cause a notice of an adjourned hearing (N58) to be issued, which has to be personally served unless an order for substituted service is obtained. Once a debtor is at court, even if after arrest (N112), the district judge may require him to complete a form of reply (N56) if he has not already done so.

23.9.2 The order

The appropriate form is an N60 or N65 (maintenance) order. On considering a debtor's income and outgoings, the proper officer or district judge fixes a 'normal deduction rate' (NDR), which is the amount to be deducted each week or month by the employer from a debtor's wages, and a 'protected earnings rate' (PER), which is the amount of the debtor's wage below which no deductions should be made. These must be specified on the form of order.

PER is usually calculated by applying allowances calculated by reference to the supplementary benefit allowances announced each year and outgoings such as rent, mortgage, rates, court orders and other significant debts. The debtor may request that the order be suspended while s/he pays the instalments ordered voluntarily. If the debtor is self-employed, the application must be dismissed. However, this does not prevent the debtor from making an instalment offer. If unemployed, the debtor's application may either be dismissed or adjourned generally, with liberty to restore. At the same time, a nominal instalment order can be made.

23.9.3   Consolidated orders

The county court makes such orders to secure the payment of a number of judgment debts. Order 27 rr 1–22 apply. An application to consolidate (N244) two or more orders may be made by any of the parties, the employer or the court of its own motion (Ord 27 r 19). Every creditor who has an attachment order against a debtor is given notice of application and a fee is payable (see below, Chapter 24).

23.9.4   Discharge or cesser of order

These are made by the court where:
- the full amount of debt has been paid;
- in maintenance cases, where payments are up to date and the NDR exceeds the rate of payments or the maintenance order ceases;
- a committal order is made (see below, 23.15);
- the debtor is not employed by the reported employer;
- the court is notified of another attachment of earnings order which is not to secure a judgment debt or an administration order;
- an administration order is made (see below, 23.14), but this can be secured by attachment order;
- a consolidated order is made;
- a debtor becomes bankrupt; and
- a court gives leave for execution to be levied.

In addition, under Ord 13, a variation order may be applied for by any party on notice.

23.9.5   Effectiveness

The pitfalls are fairly obvious, particularly if the debtor is unemployed, self-employed or changes employment without notification. However the 'teeth' attached to this method of enforcement, including the powers to arrest (N112) and commital (N59), mean that getting a response from a reluctant debtor (and employer) is not that difficult, even though it may take a little time and a little persistence.

23.10 Judgment summons

This is mainly used for enforcing maintenance orders or Inland Revenue judgments. For practice and procedure, see s 147 of the County Courts Act 1984 and CCR Ord 28) .

23.11 Garnishee proceedings

This is a procedure to seize funds held on behalf of a debtor to go toward a judgment debt, usually from monies held in a bank, building society or account at a solicitor's office (CCR Ord 30). The judgment order must be for a minimum debt of £50, although there is no maximum. Application is made without notice and the requirements on issue are:

- affidavit (N349);
- plaint note;
- fee (see below, Chapter 24);
- self-addressed envelope, if by post.

If satisfied, the district judge makes a garnishee order nisi (N84), giving a return date, which is served on the parties and on the institution, etc, where it is alleged that the monies are being held ('the garnishee'). Once served with the order, the garnishee must pay into court such monies as it holds on behalf of the debtor to go toward the judgment debt and the costs of the application. 'Deposit-taking institutions' (for example, banks and building societies) are allowed to deduct an administration fee of £30.

Notice of payment-in is sent by the court to the parties (N350 to the judgment creditor and N352 to the debtor). Where there are no monies in the account, the garnishee gives notice to the court and the creditor and proceedings are stayed, although the usual procedure is for the court to inform the parties and discharge the nisi.

On the return date, the district judge can order payment-out of monies received from the garnishee to the creditor. If there is a dispute, the district judge will either deal with the matter or give directions. If there has been no payment-in and no negative response from the garnishee, the district judge can make the order absolute.

23.11.1 Effectiveness

Although useful, this procedure cannot be used as a 'fishing' exercise. To obtain the order nisi it is necessary to convince the court that an account is being held on behalf of the debtor. However, very often it turns out that the account is overdrawn.

23.12 Charging orders

This is a procedure for imposing a charge on the beneficial interest of the debtor in land or (less commonly) securities to secure payment of a judgment debt, maintenance order or order of a tribunal. A charging order will not be granted to secure an instalment order which is not in arrears. The county court has exclusive jurisdiction to make a charging order on a High Court judgment of less than £5,000. Note that interest still continues to run on a debt of over £5,000, even if charging order proceedings are taken (Art 4 of the County Court (Interest on Judgment Debts) Order 1991 (SI 1991/1184)).

23.12.1 Requirements on issue

The provisions (generally) of CCR Ord 31 apply and the requirements on issue are:
- affidavit plus copy;
- plaint note (if county court judgment);
- fee (see below, Chapter 24); and
- self-addressed envelope, if by post.

Where a High Court order is to be enforced, additional requirements include:
- office copy judgment;
- copy of any sheriff's return; and
- details of the balance of the judgment debt outstanding.

The contents of the affidavit (CCR Ord 31 r 2) must give:
- debtor's name and address for service;
- details of any other known creditors;
- details of the subject matter of the intended charge; and
- grounds for the belief that the debtor has beneficial interest in the subject matter.

If the asset is held by a trustee, further matters need to be stated (see s 2(1)(b) of the Charging Orders Act 1979):
- where securities (other than those in court) are to be charged, giving the name and address of the person to be notified to protect the charge;
- where an interest under a trust is to be charged, giving the names and addresses of known trustees and beneficiaries;

- certifying the balance due and that the whole or any part of any instalment due remains unpaid.

If a High Court order is to be enforced, the affidavit must verify the amount due and an office copy judgment and the sheriff's return (if any) to the writ must be lodged (CCR Ord 31 r 1(2)). Where land is registered, as the Land Register is now open for inspection, office copy entries can easily be obtained by the judgment creditor and should be exhibited to the affidavit as proof of the debtor's beneficial interest in the land to be charged.

23.12.2 The charging order nisi and absolute

The district judge at first considers the application without notice and, if satisfied, makes a charging order nisi (N86) with a return date which, together with a copy of the affidavit in support, is served on the following:

- the debtor;
- where funds in court are to be charged, the Accountant General at the Funds Office;
- the debtor's other creditors named in the affidavit, unless the district judge otherwise directs;
- where a trust is involved, including where there are joint owners, one of whom is not the judgment debtor, such trustees and beneficiaries as ordered by the district judge (this can include a spouse);
- where securities not in court are to be charged, the body or persons required by RSC Ord 50 r 2(1)(b).

Service of the charging order nisi is effected (usually by post) by the creditor, not the court (see CCR Ord 31 r 1(6)–(8)) and, therefore, an affidavit of service is necessary. Service must be at least seven days before the hearing of return date. On the return date, depending on the circumstances, the court will either make the charging order absolute (N87), which is served on the parties, or discharge the nisi. If the creditor is not in a position to prove the debtor's beneficial interest because, for example, office copy entries have not been received, the court may adjourn to the first open date, ordering the nisi to continue in the meantime.

23.12.3 Protecting the charge

In the case of registered property, the nisi should be registered in the land registry as a caution and the absolute as an equitable charge. In the case of unregistered property, the nisi can be registered in the Land Charges Registry as a pending action and the absolute as an equitable charge. The district judge can add the cost of registration to the costs awarded on the absolute.

23.12.4 Effectiveness

Provided that the debtor has a valuable interest in land, there is no doubt that a charging order, particularly if followed by proceedings for sale (see below, 23.12.5), is an effective method of enforcement.

23.12.5 Enforcement by sale

The requirements on issue in proceedings for a judicial sale (CCR Ord 31 r 4) are:

- originating application plus copies for service;
- affidavit in support plus copies for service;
- fee (see below, Chapter 24); and
- self-addressed envelope, if by post.

The contents of the affidavit in support must contain:

- identification of the charging order and the property;
- the amount of charge and balance outstanding;
- verification of the debtor's title;
- identification of prior encumbrances and their amounts; and
- an estimate of the sale price.

At the hearing of the application, the district judge will decide whether an order for sale should be made, in which case the appropriate directions will be given (see below, Chapter 24) or whether any other appropriate order should be made for payment of the judgment debt. Where land is owned by more than one person, of whom at least one is not the debtor, the charge can only be enforced by the appointment of a receiver under CCR Ord 32 or by order for sale under s 14 of the Trusts of Land and Appointment of Trustees Act 1996 (see also PD40D, para 2).

23.12.6 Effectiveness

The main drawback with enforcement by sale is where the equity in the property, after deducting all prior encumbrances, is not enough to meet the charge.

23.13 Receivers

A general power is given to the county court to appoint a receiver. The procedure is outlined in detail in CCR Ord 32.

23.14 Administration orders

Where a debtor owes several debts which together do not exceed £5,000, the court may make an administration order, which provides for payment of the total debts by single instalments which are then divided among the creditors (CCR Ord 39). The court may also consider a 'composition' order (so much in the £).

The requirements on issue for such an order are:

- request (N92) which lists the creditors, the amount of each debt and also contains a statement of means;
- fee (see below, Chapter 24); and
- self-addressed envelope, if by post.

Notice of the application is sent to the creditors (N373).

At the hearing, the district judge, if satisfied that an order should be made, fixes the amount of the instalment which can be secured by an attachment of earnings order (see 13.9). The order may be reviewed, varied, suspended or revoked.

23.14.1 Effectiveness

An administration order is also known as 'the poor man's bankruptcy' and is certainly useful where a debtor has several debts. From the creditors' point of view, however, it may be a long time before the debts are finally extinguished.

23.15 Committal

23.15.1 For non-attendance

A warrant for committal may be issued for non-attendance by the debtor at an adjourned hearing of:

- judgment summons (N70);
- attachment of earnings (N59);
- oral examination (CCR Ord 25 r 3(5)).

Alternatively, the court may order the debtor to be arrested and brought before a judge (N112). The warrant may be suspended before execution on request by the creditor or the debtor.

23.15.2 For breach of an order or undertaking

CCR Ord 29 applies, and the requirements are as follows:

- the judgment or order must have been served (together with any appropriate penal notice) on the recipient (CCR Ord 29 r 1(2), (3)) or the judge must be satisfied that the recipient is aware of the order (CCR Ord 29 r 1(6));

- the order must have been served in time for it to be obeyed within the time limit allowed (CCR Ord 29 r 1(2)(b));

- a notice of application for committal (N78) must be served personally, unless this is dispensed with (Ord 29 r 1(4), (7), (8)), at least two clear days before the return date (Ord 13 r 1(2)).

Important points

- An undertaking given by a party in person is usually enforceable as if it were a court order (N117).

- A committal order for breach must strictly follow wording of N79.

- A committal order must be served on the recipient either before or at the execution of the warrant, unless the judge orders otherwise (Ord 29 r 1(5)).

- Imprisonment is for up to two years, but this can be suspended on conditions or a fine substituted or added.

- A person arrested under warrant is imprisoned until he/she purges contempt on a written application or the term of imprisonment expires (Ord 29 r 3).

23.15.3 Contempt of court

Any person who assaults any officer of the court or anyone insulting a juror, a witness or an officer of the court, either while at the court or when going to or from the court, or for interrupting court proceedings or misbehaving in court, may either be committed to prison for up to one month or fined up to a maximum of £2,500 (s 118(1) of the 1984 Act).

Any person assaulting a court officer while in the execution of his duty is liable to up to three months' imprisonment and/or a fine up to £5,000 (s 14 of the 1984 Act). The power to commit or fine under this section may be exercised by a circuit or district judge. A person rescuing or attempting to rescue goods seized under a county court execution is liable to up to one month's imprisonment and/or a fine up to £2,500 (s 92 of the 1984 Act).

23.15.4 Effectiveness

The effect of committal is obvious. However, it is only resorted to when all other forms of enforcement have failed, and in debt claims committal does not pay the debt, although the threat of it may encourage a debtor to be co-operative.

23.16 Enforcement outside England and Wales

The enforcement of county court judgments outside England and Wales (as well as outside the UK) is fully outlined in *The County Court Practice*, CCR Ord 35.

24 Appendix

24.1 N1 Part 7 claim form

	In the	
Claim Form		
	Claim No.	

Claimant

SEAL

Defendant(s)

Brief details of claim

Value

Defendant's name and address		Amount claimed	
		Court fee	
		Solicitor's costs	
		Total amount	
		Issue date	

£

The court office at

is open between 10 am and 4 pm Monday to Friday. When corresponding with the court, please address forms or letters to the Court Manager and quote the claim number.

N1 Claim form (CPR Part 7) (10.00)

Printed on behalf of The Court Service

| | Claim No. | | | | | |

Does, or will, your claim include any issues under the Human Rights Act 1998?   ☐ Yes   ☐ No

Particulars of Claim (attached)(to follow)

Statement of Truth
*(I believe)(The Claimant believes) that the facts stated in these particulars of claim are true.
*I am duly authorised by the claimant to sign this statement

Full name _____

Name of claimant's solicitor's firm _____

signed _____ position or office held _____
*(Claimant)(Litigation friend)(Claimant's solicitor)   (if signing on behalf of firm or company)
*delete as appropriate

Claimant's or claimant's solicitor's address to
which documents or payments should be sent if
different from overleaf including (if appropriate)
details of DX, fax or e-mail.

24.2 N208 Part 8 claim form

<table>
<tr><td colspan="2">Claim Form
(CPR Part 8)</td><td colspan="2">In the</td></tr>
<tr><td colspan="2"></td><td colspan="2">Claim No.</td></tr>
</table>

Claimant

SEAL

Defendant(s)

Does your claim include any issues under the Human Rights Act 1998? ☐ Yes ☐ No

Details of claim *(see also overleaf)*

£

Defendant's name and address		Court fee	
		Solicitor's costs	
		Issue date	

The court office at

is open between 10 am and 4 pm Monday to Friday. When corresponding with the court, please address forms or letters to the Court Manager and quote the case number.

N208 Claim form (CPR Part 8) (10.00)   *Printed on behalf of The Court Service*

	Claim No.						

Details of claim *(continued)*

Statement of Truth

*(I believe)(The Claimant believes) that the facts stated in these particulars of claim are true.

* I am duly authorised by the claimant to sign this statement

Full name _____

Name of claimant's solicitor's firm _____

signed_____ position or office held_____

*(Claimant)(Litigation friend)(Claimant's solicitor) (if signing on behalf of firm or company)

delete as appropriate

Claimant's or claimant's solicitor's address to which documents should be sent if different from overleaf. If you are prepared to accept service by DX, fax or e-mail, please add details.

24.3 N9B defence and counterclaim

Defence and Counterclaim (specified amount)

- Fill in this form if you wish to dispute all or part of the claim and/or make a claim against the claimant (counterclaim).
- You have a limited number of days to complete and return this form to the court.
- Before completing this form, please read the notes for guidance attached to the claim form.
- Please ensure that all boxes at the top right of this form are completed. You can obtain the correct names and number from the claim form. The court cannot trace your case without this information.

How to fill in this form

- Complete sections 1 and 2. Tick the correct boxes and give the other details asked for.
- Set out your defence in section 3. If necessary continue on a separate piece of paper making sure that the claim number is clearly shown on it. In your defence you must state which allegations in the particulars of claim you deny and your reasons for doing so. **If you fail to deny an allegation it may be taken that you admit it.**
- If you dispute only some of the allegations you must
  - specify which you admit and which you deny, and
  - give your own version of events if different from the claimant's.

In the	
Claim No.	
Claimant (including ref)	
Defendant	

- If you wish to make a claim against the claimant (a counterclaim) complete section 4.
- Complete and sign section 5 before sending this form to the court. Keep a copy of the claim form and this form.

Community Legal Service Fund (CLSF)

You may qualify for assistance from the CLSF (this used to be called 'legal aid') to meet some or all of your legal costs. Ask about the CLSF at any county court office or any information or help point which displays this logo.

---

1. How much of the claim do you dispute?

☐ I dispute the full amount claimed as shown on the claim form

or

☐ I admit the amount of £ _____

If you dispute only part of the claim you must **either**:

- pay the amount admitted to the person named at the address for payment on the claim form (see How to Pay in the notes on the back of, or attached to, the claim form). Then send this defence to the court

or

- complete the admission form **and** this defence form and send them to the court.

☐ I paid the amount admitted on (date) _____

or

☐ I enclose the completed form of admission (go to section 2)

2. Do you dispute this claim because you have already paid it? Tick whichever applies

☐ No (go to section 3)

☐ Yes   I paid £ _____ to the claimant

on _____ (before the claim form was issued)

Give details of where and how you paid it in the box below (then go to section 3)

---

3. Defence

Defence (continued)   Claim No. [   ]

4. If you wish to make a claim against the claimant (a counterclaim)

If your claim is for a specific sum of money, how much are you claiming? £ [   ]

- To start your counterclaim, you will have to pay a fee. Court staff will tell you how much you have to pay

My claim is for *(please specify nature of claim)*

[   ]

- You may not be able to make a counterclaim where the claimant is the Crown (e.g. a Government Department). Ask at your local county court office for further information.

What are your reasons for making the counterclaim?
If you need to continue on a separate sheet put the claim number in the top right hand corner

[   ]

5. Signed

(To be signed by you or by your solicitor or litigation friend)

*(I believe)(The defendant believes) that the facts stated in this form are true. *I am duly authorised by the defendant to sign this statement.

delete as appropriate

Position or office held
(if signing on behalf of firm or company)

[   ]

Date [   ]

Give an address to which notices about this case can be sent to you

[   ]
Postcode

Tel. no. [   ]

	if applicable
fax no.	
DX no.	
e-mail	

24.4 N150 allocation questionnaire

Allocation questionnaire

To be completed by, or on behalf of,

In the

who is [1ˢᵗ][2ⁿᵈ][3ʳᵈ][ ][Claimant][Defendant]
[Part 20 claimant] in this claim

Claim No.

Last date for filing
with court office

Please read the notes on page five before completing the questionnaire.

You should note the date by which it must be returned and the name of the court it should be returned to since this may be different from the court where the proceedings were issued.

If you have settled this claim (or if you settle it on a future date) and do not need to have it heard or tried, you must let the court know immediately.

Have you sent a copy of this completed form to the other party(ies)? ☐ Yes ☐ No

A Settlement

Do you wish there to be a one month stay to attempt to settle the claim, either by informal discussion or by alternative dispute resolution? ☐ Yes ☐ No

B Location of trial

Is there any reason why your claim needs to be heard at a particular court? ☐ Yes ☐ No

If Yes, say which court and why?

C Pre-action protocols

If an approved pre-action protocol applies to this claim, complete **Part 1** only. If not, complete **Part 2** only. If you answer 'No' to the question in either Part 1 or 2, please explain the reasons why on a separate sheet and attach it to this questionnaire.

Part 1   The* _____ protocol applies to this claim.

*please say
which
protocol*

Have you complied with it? ☐ Yes ☐ No

Part 2   No pre-action protocol applies to this claim.

Have you exchanged information and/or documents (evidence) with the other party in order to assist in settling the claim? ☐ Yes ☐ No

N150 Allocation questionnaire (11.00)   I   *Printed on behalf of The Court Service*

D   Case management information

What amount of the claim is in dispute?   £ _____

Applications

Have you made any application(s) in this claim?   ☐ Yes   ☐ No

If Yes, what for?   _____   For hearing on _____
(e.g. summary judgment,
add another party)

Witnesses

So far as you know at this stage, what witnesses of fact do you intend to call at the trial or final hearing including, if appropriate, yourself?

Witness name	Witness to which facts

Experts

Do you wish to use expert evidence at the trial or final hearing?   ☐ Yes   ☐ No

Have you already copied any experts' report(s) to the   ☐ None yet   ☐ Yes   ☐ No
other party(ies)?   obtained

Do you consider the case suitable for a single joint expert in any field?   ☐ Yes   ☐ No

Please list any single joint experts you propose to use and any other experts you wish to rely on. Identify single joint experts with the initials 'SJ' after their name(s).

Expert's name	Field of expertise (eg. orthopaedic surgeon, surveyor, engineer)

Do you want your expert(s) to give evidence orally at the trial or final hearing?   ☐ Yes   ☐ No

If Yes, give the reasons why you think oral evidence is necessary:

continue over ⬛➡

Track

Which track do you consider is most suitable for your claim? Tick one box
☐ small claims track ☐ fast track ☐ multi-track

If you have indicated a track which would not be the normal track for the claim, please give brief reasons for your choice

E Trial or final hearing

How long do you estimate the trial or final hearing will take?
____days ____hours ____minutes

Are there any days when you, an expert or an essential witness will not be able to attend court for the trial or final hearing?
☐ Yes ☐ No

If Yes, please give details

Name	Dates not available

F Proposed directions *(Parties should agree directions wherever possible)*

Have you attached a list of the directions you think appropriate for the management of the claim?
☐ Yes ☐ No

If Yes, have they been agreed with the other party(ies)?
☐ Yes ☐ No

G Costs

*Do **not** complete this section if you have suggested your case is suitable for the small claims track **or** you have suggested one of the other tracks and you do not have a solicitor acting for you.*

What is your estimate of your costs incurred to date?
£

What do you estimate your overall costs are likely to be?
£

In substantial cases these questions should be answered in compliance with CPR Part 43

H Other information

Have you attached documents to this questionnaire? ☐ Yes ☐ No

Have you sent these documents to the other party(ies)? ☐ Yes ☐ No

If Yes, when did they receive them?

Do you intend to make any applications in the immediate future? ☐ Yes ☐ No

If Yes, what for?

In the space below, set out any other information you consider will help the judge to manage the claim.

Signed _____   Date _____

[Counsel][Solicitor][for the][1st][2nd][3rd][   ]
[Claimant][Defendant][Part 20 claimant]

Please enter your firm's name, reference number and full postal address including (if appropriate) details of DX, fax or e-mail

	if applicable	
	fax no.	
	DX no.	
Tel. no. Postcode	e-mail	
Your reference no.		

Notes for completing an allocation questionnaire

- If the claim is not settled, a judge must allocate it to an appropriate case management track. To help the judge choose the most just and cost-effective track, you must now complete the attached questionnaire.
- If you fail to return the allocation questionnaire by the date given, the judge may make an order which leads to your claim or defence being struck out, or hold an allocation hearing. If there is an allocation hearing the judge may order any party who has not filed their questionnaire to pay, immediately, the costs of that hearing.
- Use a separate sheet if you need more space for your answers marking clearly which section the information refers to. You should write the claim number on it, and on any other documents you send with your allocation questionnaire. Please ensure they are firmly attached to it.
- The letters below refer to the sections of the questionnaire and tell you what information is needed.

A Settlement

If you think that you and the other party may be able to negotiate a settlement you should tick the 'Yes' box. The court may order a stay, whether or not all the other parties to the claim agree. You should still complete the rest of the questionnaire, even if you are requesting a stay. Where a stay is granted it will be for an initial period of one month. You may settle the claim either by informal discussion with the other party or by alternative dispute resolution (ADR). ADR covers a range of different processes which can help settle disputes. More information is available in the booklet 'Resolving Disputes Without Going To Court' available from every county court office.

B Location of trial

High Court cases are usually heard at the Royal Courts of Justice or certain Civil Trial Centres. Fast or multi-track trials may be dealt with at a Civil Trial Centre or at the court where the claim is proceeding. Small claim cases are usually heard at the court in which they are proceeding.

C Pre-action protocols

Before any claim is started, the court expects you to have exchanged information and documents relevant to the claim, to assist in settling it. For some types of claim e.g. personal injury, there are approved protocols that should have been followed.

D Case management information

Applications

It is important for the court to know if you have already made any applications in the claim, what they are for and when they will be heard. The outcome of the applications may affect the case management directions the court gives.

Witnesses

Remember to include yourself as a witness of fact, if you will be giving evidence.

Experts

Oral or written expert evidence will only be allowed at the trial or final hearing with the court's permission. The judge will decide what permission it seems appropriate to give when the claim is allocated to track. Permission in small claims track cases will only be given exceptionally.

Track

The basic guide by which claims are normally allocated to a track is the amount in dispute, although other factors such as the complexity of the case will also be considered. A leaflet available from the court office explains the limits in greater detail.

Small Claims track	Disputes valued at not more than £5,000 except
	· those including a claim for personal injuries worth over £1,000 and
	· those for housing disrepair where either the cost of repairs or other work exceeds £1,000 or any other claim for damages exceeds £1,000
Fast track	Disputes valued at more than £5,000 but not more than £15,000
Multi-track	Disputes over £15,000

E Trial or final hearing

You should enter only those dates when you, your expert(s) or essential witness(es) will not be able to attend court because of holiday or other committments.

F Proposed directions

Attach the list of directions, if any, you believe will be appropriate to be given for the management of the claim. Agreed directions on fast and multi-track cases should be based on the forms of standard directions set out in the practice direction to CPR Part 28 and form PF52.

G Costs

Only complete this section if you are a solicitor and have suggested the claim is suitable for allocation to the fast or multi-track.

H Other Information

Answer the questions in this section. Decide if there is any other information you consider will help the judge to manage the claim. Give details in the space provided referring to any documents you have attached to support what you are saying.

24.5   N170 listing questionnaire

Listing questionnaire

In the

Claim No.

Last date for filing
with court office

To

- The court will use the information which you and the other party(ies) provide to fix a date for trial (or to confirm the date and time if one has already been fixed), to confirm the estimated length of trial and to set a timetable for the trial itself. In multi-track cases the court will also decide whether to hold a pre-trial review.

- If you do not complete and return the questionnaire the procedural judge may
  - make an order which leads to your statement of case (claim or defence) being struck out.
  - decide to hold a listing hearing. You may be ordered to pay (immediately) the other parties' costs of attending.
  - if there is sufficient information, list the case for trial and give any appropriate directions.

- Separate estimates of costs incurred to date and those which will be incurred if the case proceeds to trial, should be given using Form 1 in the Schedule of Costs Forms set out in the Civil Procedure Rules. This form should be attached to and returned with your completed questionnaire. (This relates only to costs incurred by legal representatives.)

A Directions complied with

1. Have you complied with all the previous directions given by the court?   ☐ Yes   ☐ No

2. If no, please explain which directions are outstanding and why

Directions outstanding	Reasons directions outstanding

3. Are any further directions required to prepare the case for trial?   ☐ Yes   ☐ No
   (If no go to section B)

4. If yes, please explain directions required and give reasons

Directions required	Reasons required

B Experts

1. Has the court already given permission for you to use written expert evidence? ☐ Yes ☐ No
(If no go to section B6)

2. If yes, please give name and field of expertise.

Name of expert	Whether joint expert (please tick, if appropriate)	Field of expertise

3. Have the expert(s') report(s) been agreed with the other parties? ☐ Yes ☐ No

4. Have the experts met to discuss their reports? ☐ Yes ☐ No

5. Has the court already given permission for the expert(s) to give oral evidence at the trial? (If yes go to Q8) ☐ Yes ☐ No

6. If no, are you seeking that permission? (If yes go to Q7) ☐ Yes ☐ No
(If no go to section C)

7. Give your reasons for seeking permission.

8. What are the names, addresses and fields of expertise of your experts?

Expert 1	Expert 2	Expert 3	Expert 4

9. Please give details of any dates within the trial period when your expert(s) will not be available.

Name of expert	Dates not available

C Other witnesses

(If you are not calling other witnesses go to section D)

1. How many other witnesses (including yourself) will be giving evidence on your behalf at the trial? (do not include experts – see section B above)

(Give number)

2. What are the names and addresses of your witnesses?

Witness 1	Witness 2	Witness 3	Witness 4

3. Please give details of any dates within the trial period when you or your witnesses will not be available?

Name of witness	Dates not available

4. Are any of the witness statements agreed? ☐ Yes ☐ No
(If no go to Q6)

5. If yes, give the name of the witness and the date of his or her statement

Name of witness	Date of statement

6. Do you or any of your witnesses need any special facilities? ☐ Yes ☐ No
(If no go to Q8)

7. If yes, what are they?

8. Will any of your witnesses be provided with an interpreter? ☐ Yes ☐ No
(If no go to section D)

9. If yes, say what type of interpreter e.g. language (stating which), deaf/blind etc.

D Legal representation

1. Who will be presenting your case at the hearing or trial? ☐ You ☐ Solicitor ☐ Counsel

2. Please give details of any dates within the trial period when the person presenting your case will not be available.

Name	Dates not available

E Other matters

1. How long do you estimate the trial will take, including cross-examination and closing arguments?

Minutes	Hours	Days

If your case is allocated to the fast track the maximum time allowed for the whole case will be no more than one day.

2. What is the estimated number of pages of evidence to be included in the trial bundle?

(please give number)

Fast track cases only

3. The court will normally give you 3 weeks notice in the fast track of the date fixed for a fast track trial unless, in exceptional circumstances, the court directs that shorter notice will be given. Would you be prepared to accept shorter notice of the date fixed for trial? ☐ Yes ☐ No

Signed

Claimant/defendant or Counsel/Solicitor for the claimant/defendant

Date

24.6   Form H costs estimate

Ancillary Relief
Costs Estimate of
[Applicant]
[Respondent]

In the	
	County Court
Case No. Always quote this	
Applicant's Solicitor's reference	
Respondent's Solicitor's reference	

The marriage of **John Smith** and **Samantha Smith**

PART 1

	Legal Aid Rates £	Indemnity Rate £
1. Ancillary relief solicitor's costs (including VAT) including costs of the current hearing, and any previous solicitor's costs		
2. Disbursements (include VAT, if appropriate, and any incurred by previous solicitors)		
3. All Counsel's fees (including VAT)		
TOTAL		

PART 2

4. Add any private cases costs previously incurred (Legal Aid cases only)		
5. GRAND TOTAL		

PART 3

6. State what has been paid towards the total at 5 above		
7. Amount of any contributions paid by the assisted person towards their legal aid certificate		

NB.   If you are Legally Aided and might be seeking an order for costs against the other party complete both rates

Dated

The court office at

Is open between 10 am and 4 pm Monday to Friday. When corresponding with the court, please address forms or letters to the Court Manager and quote the case number. If you do not do so, your correspondence may be returned.

Form H Costs Estimate

24.7 County Court Fees Order 1999 (SI 1999/689) – Schedule – Table of Fees

The Court Service

County Court Fees

Fees you will have to pay to issue a claim, enforce judgment or to make applications
This leaflet does not include fees for family cases

**from
2nd October 2000**

Please make all cheques payable to
HM Paymaster General
(HMPG)

Starting your claim

◯ To issue a claim form where your claim is for money only and the amount is not more than:

£200	£27
£300	£38
£400	£50
£500	£60
£1,000	£80
£5,000	£115
£15,000	£230
£50,000	£350
£50,000+	£500
For an unlimited amount	£500

◯ To issue proceedings where your claim is for something other than money £120

Counterclaim

◯ To make a claim against the claimant (a 'counterclaim') the fees above apply; that is, the fee to be paid depends on the amount of the counterclaim.

Preparing for trial

Allocation
- claims for money of £1,000 or less no fee
- all other claims   £80

Note: This fee is payable by the claimant except where the case is proceeding on a counterclaim alone, when it is payable by the defendant. The fee must be paid when the allocation questionnaire is filed.

If either:
* the court decides that an allocation questionnaire is not required; or
* the Rules do not require an allocation questionnaire to be completed,

where applicable the fee must be paid:
* within 28 days of filing the defence; or
* on the filing of the last defence if there is more than one defendant; or
* within 28 days of expiry of the time for filing all defences.

Warning: If you do not pay the allocation fee when required, the court can make an order which may lead to your statement of case (claim or counterclaim) being 'struck out'. This would mean that you could not proceed with your claim (or counterclaim).

Appeals
To file an appellant's or a respondent's notice if permission to appeal or an extension of time to appeal (or both) is applied for, when the appeal is against a decision made in:

- the small claims track   £100
- any other appeal   £150

Note: If the court **refuses** either your application for permission to appeal or for an extension of time in which to appeal, £50 (small claims appeals) or £100 (other appeals) will be refunded to you

To file an appellant's or a respondent's notice if permission to appeal is not required or permission has already been given by the lower court, when the appeal is against a decision made in:

- the small claims track   £50
- any other appeal   £100

No fee is payable on the filing of a **respondent's notice** where the respondent is asking the appeal court to uphold the lower court's order for the reasons already given

Trial fee
- multi-track cases   £300
- other cases*   £200

*Does not include cases in the small claims track.

Note: The trial fee is payable by the claimant except where the case is proceeding on a counterclaim alone, when it is payable by the defendant. The fee must be paid on the filing of the listing questionnaire.

If the court fixes the trial date or trial week without a listing questionnaire, the fee must be paid within 14 days of:
* the despatch of notice of the trial date or trial week; or, if no written notice is given,
* the date when you are told the trial date or trial week.

Where the court receives notice, **in writing**:
* before the trial date has been fixed; or
* if it has been fixed, at least seven days before the day on which the trial is due to begin,

that the case has been settled or discontinued, the trial fee will be refunded.

Warning: If you do not pay the trial fee when required, the court can make an order which may lead to your statement of case (claim or counterclaim) being 'struck out'. This would mean that you could not proceed with your claim (or counterclaim).

Applications
- To apply for judgment to be set aside   £50
- To apply to vary a judgment or suspend enforcement   £25
- To make an application on notice   £50
- To apply for a summons or order for a witness to attend   £30
- To apply by consent, or without notice, for a judgment or order. **This does not include requests for judgment on admission or in default for which no fee is payable**   £25

Assessment of costs
- To request a detailed assessment hearing: Community Legal Service Fund only (no order for payment by another party)   £80
  other   £150
- To appeal against detailed assessment   £50
- To issue a default costs certificate   £40
- To apply to set aside a default costs certificate   £50

To apply for approval of Community
Legal Service Assessment Certificate   £20

Enforcing Judgments

If the court has ordered some one to pay you
a sum of money or to return your goods or
property and they have not done so, you can issue
enforcement proceedings. Details about
enforcement are available from the court in a free
set of leaflets.

To issue a warrant of execution to recover a sum of
money:
- where the sum recovered is
  not more than £125   £25
- where the sum to be recovered
  is more than £125   £45
- To issue a warrant for recovery
  of land or property (possession)   £80

Note: Where a warrant for recovery of land or
goods also includes a claim for money, no
additional fee is payable.

- To issue a warrant of delivery   £80

- To reissue a warrant of execution at
  a new address, except a further attempt
  at enforcement following suspension   £20

Attachment of earnings

- To issue an application for an
  attachment of earnings order   £50

On a consolidated attachment of earnings order,
for every £1, or part of a £1, of the money paid
into court, a fee of 10p is deducted from the
money before it is paid out to you.

Charging orders

- To issue an application for
  a charging order   £50

Garnishee orders

- To issue an application for
  a garnishee order   £50

Judgment summonses

- To issue an application for
  a judgment summons   £80

Oral examination

- To issue an application for an
  oral examination   £40

Registering tribunal awards

- To register an award (for example,
  of a tribunal) for enforcement   £30

Copies of documents
A fee is charged for making photocopies in the court
office

Documents held by the court
- for photocopy of first page of document: £1
- for photocopy of each subsequent page of
  the same document: 20p per sheet
- any additional photocopies of the whole
  document: 20p per sheet

Documents supplied by you at the time of copying
- for each photocopy: 20p per sheet

For copies of documents provided on computer disk or
other electronic form: £3 per copy.

Registration of county court judgments
- To ask for a certificate of
  satisfaction or a request for
  cancellation when a debt is paid   £10

Bankruptcy and company winding up
- To issue a bankruptcy petition for your
  own affairs (debtor's petition)   £120

- To issue a bankruptcy petition
  against someone who owes you
  money (creditor's petition)   £150
- To issue a petition to wind up
  a company which owes you money   £150

- Request for a certificate of
  discharge from bankruptcy   £50 and
  £1 for each copy after the first certificate

What if I cannot afford the fee?
If you are an individual and not represented by a
solicitor under Community Legal Service, you may **not**
have to pay a fee if you are receiving:
- income support;
- income-based jobseeker's allowance;
- the **maximum** Working Families Tax Credit (WFTC)
  or Disabled Person's Tax Credit (DPTC);
- WFTC or DPTC where £71.10 or less per week has
  been deducted from the maximum credit;
- Legal Help, through a solicitor, **and** in receipt of one
  of the above benefits.

Otherwise, if you can show that the payment of a fee
would involve undue hardship to you, the Court
Manager may reduce the fee or 'remit' (say you do not
have to pay) the fee.

You will need to give proof of your financial
circumstances.

If you are not sure whether you qualify for a reduction
of the fee, or you are exempt from paying a fee, court
staff will be able to advise you. Ask the court for a Form
EX160 *Application for a fee exemption or remission*. You
will have to make a separate application for each fee
that you have to pay.

Ex50 Fees (1.0.00)